PUBLICATIONS OF THE DEPARTMENT OF
ROMANCE LANGUAGES
UNIVERSITY OF NORTH CAROLINA

General Editor: ALDO SCAGLIONE

NORTH CAROLINA STUDIES IN THE
ROMANCE LANGUAGES AND LITERATURES

ESSAYS; TEXTS, TEXTUAL STUDIES AND TRANSLATIONS; SYMPOSIA

Founder: URBAN TIGNER HOLMES

Editor: JUAN BAUTISTA AVALLE-ARCE
Associate Editor: FREDERICK W. VOGLER

Other publications of the Department: *Estudios de Hispanófila, Hispanófila, Romance Notes, Studia Raeto-Romanica*

Distributed by:

INTERNATIONAL SCHOLARLY BOOK SERVICE, INC.

P. O. BOX 4347
Portland, Oregon   97208
U. S. A.

NORTH CAROLINA STUDIES IN THE
ROMANCE LANGUAGES AND LITERATURES:
Number 140

VISUAL VARIETY AND SPATIAL GRANDEUR

VISUAL VARIETY AND SPATIAL GRANDEUR

A STUDY OF THE TRANSITION FROM THE SIXTEENTH TO THE SEVENTEENTH CENTURY IN FRANCE

BY

JOHN F. WINTER

CHAPEL HILL

NORTH CAROLINA STUDIES IN THE
ROMANCE LANGUAGES AND LITERATURES
U.N.C. DEPARTMENT OF ROMANCE LANGUAGES
1974

Library of Congress Cataloging in Publication Data

Winter, John F.
    Visual Variety and Spatial Grandeur.

    (North Carolina Studies in the Romance Languages and Literatures)
        1. Space (Art). 2. Arts, Renaissance—France. 3. Arts, Baroque—France. 4. Arts—France. I. Title. II. Series.
NX549.A1W56   700'.944   74-10611
ISBN 0-88438-940-5

ISBN 978-0-8078-9140-7

DEPÓSITO LEGAL: V. 2.038 - 1974

ARTES GRÁFICAS SOLER, S. A. - JÁVEA, 28 - VALENCIA (8) - 1974

To my father

TABLE OF CONTENTS

ILLUSTRATIONS

ACKNOWLEDGMENT

At the completion of my work I wish to express my gratitude to a number of friends and institutions that contributed in some way to the genesis of this book. The idea on which it is based germinated during my Princeton graduate studies, particularly under the influence of Professor Gilbert Chinard's stimulating lectures on sensualism and an oral report given by my fellow student Rudolf Treo. For my historical approach I am deeply indebted to Professor Américo, for my sporting attitude to the subject matter and my relatively tolerant reaction to other critics — as far as these virtues are discernible at all in my writings — to the splendid example of Professor Ira Wade. Professor Helmut Hatzfeld opened my eyes to the possibility of parallel studies between literature and the arts. As for my familiarity with the history of art, it goes back to my studies at the University of Vienna, and particularly to the animated lectures of Professor Sedlmayer. For this part of my study I also must express my thanks to the excellent librarians of the Fine Arts Section of the New York Public Library and especially to Miss Jeanette Byrne who has a position in the Metropolitan Museum of New York and who graciously consented to review the first version of my chapter on French paintings. For a first introduction of my theme to the public I am obliged to the Modern Language Association of America and the New York Renaissance Club that repeatedly offered me the possibility to read papers, and also to a number of periodicals that published articles derived from these papers, especially *Symposium* and the *Romanic Review*. I also must refer with gratitude to the grants I received from the Philosophical Society of America, from Fordham University, from the Charles Phelps Taft Memorial Fund and Dr. Wessel's special fund, both at the University of Cincinnati. I may add that I could have never finished the book without the sabbatical leaves offered to me by Fordham University and the University of Cincinnati. Last but not least let me mention my numerous benefactors, my friends Otto Hoffman, Ing. Hugo Meguscher, Ferdinand Bartak, my brother Paul and his wife Clara, Peggy Rath and Alphonsus Dietsohe, who at difficult periods of my life gave me encouragement and stimulated my thought. My special thanks are due to my late father who taught me never to give up my objectives, to my unforgettable mother who gave me some of her sensitivity and sense of humour, and to my wife Alice, my assiduous collaborator and my Muse.

PREFACE

The subject matter of this book is a momentous metamorphosis that took place in the visual outlook on the world in France between the fifteenth and the middle of the seventeenth century. The cozy milieu within the limits of which the medieval man contemplated his existence kept growing in size until it reached cosmic proportions. And spatial expansion went hand in hand with an increasing pleasure taken in variety, [1] the twin expression of the general drive towards the amplification of visual realities. Just as striking is the reaction that sets in against these tendencies in the early part of the seventeenth century. The esthetic ideal of the new era materializes in the diminution or dimming or the abstract presentation of space and in a general aversion against multifariousness. We therefore have here a cycle within the evolution of history marked by the broadening and narrowing of sensual experience.

Our study of this material embraces literature, the arts and to some extent the sciences as well. In an introductory passage we will deal with the Renaissance concept of space as a general European phenomenon. The growth and the full materialization of spatial grandeur and variety in France then will be investigated first in painting and then in literature. In the latter, special attention will be given to Lemaire de Belges, Rabelais and Ronsard in whose works French Renaissance imagery reaches its climax. The conclusion will point to the decline of both space and variety in the first part of the seventeenth century.

It should be noted that our study, a first attempt to probe into the field of French Renaissance imagery in an integrated form, touches

---

[1] Helmut Hatzfeld, *Literature through Art* (New York, 1952).

on a controversial point of literary criticism. The richness and amplitude found in the literature of this era is admired as well as censured
as a form of intellectual dissipation. Some of the most enthusiastic
French commentators of Rabelais and Ronsard object to a lack of
restraint in these authors. [2] Yet with all due respect for the beatuy
and the intellectual excellence found in the temperate mode of expression of more modern French writings, it is our contention that
the "pre-Boileau" style which opposes that trend is highly accom-
plished and must be measured with a yardstick of its own. [3] Our analysis will show that the genius of France is able to operate on a variety
of planes.

---

[2] "Rabelais ignore ces qualités qui seront portées à leur apogée cent ans
plus tard: l'ordre, la symétrie, la netteté de la composition" and "ce qui
rompt l'équilibre... c'est bien souvent l'étalage de l'érudition." Jean Plattard,
La vie et l'œuvre de Rabelais (Paris, 1939), p. 92. Gustave Cohen quotes
passages from Ronsard in order to criticize him: "Pourquoi, au lieu d'imiter
seulement 'les saintes conceptions de Pindare', a-t-il voulu aussi, lui Français,
né pour l'ordre, imiter 'ses admirables inconstances', entendez son désordre,
'brouillans ores ceci, ores cela'." Ronsard, sa vie et son œuvre (Paris, 1956),
p. 88. "Toutes les fois qu'il a le souci de peindre, nous retrouvons cette
superfluité, cette surabondance... d'un art orgueilleux et encore naïf...."
Henri Franchet, Le poète et son œuvre d'après Ronsard (Paris, 1923), p. 214.
[3] Raymond Lebègue, Ronsard, l'homme et l'œuvre (Paris, 1950), p. 23.

INFATUATION WITH SPACE

The Renaissance is fascinated by distance, by distance in time as well as in space. It reaches out for remote parts of history and the universe. Its passionate interest for antiquity and the cosmos distinguishes it from the Middle Ages with which a trend in historical studies has striven to confuse it. [4]

Pleasure taken in the penetration of space is responsible for exceptional progress made during the Ranaissance in three great domains, in geography, in astronomy and the fine arts. The search for the African West Coast, the circumnavigation of the Cape of Good Hope, the crossing of the Indian Ocean as well as the westward travels that lead to the discovery of a new continent and the first trip around the globe derive from the same impulsion as the observation of the sky by astronomers, their study of the solstice, of the equinoxes and their procession, of the obliquity of the ecliptic, of the position and motion of the comets, of the earthshine, of the homocentric spheres, and the density of the celestial ether, all of which leads in its final effect to the discovery of the heliocentric system. [5] While the maritime voyagers, particularly those of Portugal and Spain are well known, most of us are far less aware of the accomplishments of some excellent fifteenth and sixteenth century astronomers, of Toscanelli, Fracastaro, Maurolico, Peter Bienewitz (Apianus), George

---

[4] W. K. Ferguson, *Tre Renaissance in Historical Thought* (New York, 1948), pp. 293-373.

[5] Giorgio Abetti, *The History of Astronomy*, trans. Betty Burr Abetti (New York, 1952), pp. 52-63.

Purbach and Johann Muller (Regiomontanus). [6] They laid the ground-work to the universally recognized works of Copernicus and Tycho Brahe.

The artist responds to the general tendency in his own way. The painter's eye moves from the plane into space in order to create three-dimensional vistas with large volumes. [7] He studies the rules of perspective, experiments with foreshortened frontal and oblique set-tings, and produces in one of his boldest schemes, in illusionism, a system in which the vanishing point not being focused on any single object, the spectator receives a visual impression of infinity. [8] The architects are concerned with the harmonious distribution of ample volumes. The sculptor develops a special feel for space, a plastic sensibility new in the history of art that Herbert Read called "the synthetic realization of the mass and the ponderability of an object". [9]

Its artistic manifestations show clearly that the concept of space turned into an ideal. It is interesting to observe in this respect that even scientific studies of the earth and the universe acquire during the Renaissance esthetic attributes. While carefully measuring the po-sition of heavenly bodies with their gnomons, astrolabes, quadrants, sextants, armillae etc., while improving the tables and struggling with mechanics, the astronomers were awestruck by the beatuy of the cos-mos. In a Platonic mood reminiscent of Pico della Mirandola, Coper-nicus calls God an artist, the best and most perfect of them all. Nothing is as beautiful as the sky, he exclaims, and the very words *mundus* and *coelum* well express it, the former meaning perfection of form, the latter indicating purity and ornament. Because of its splen-dor most philosophers called the sky the visible God, Copernicus adds, and if the dignity of the arts were evaluated by the matter they deal with, astronomy should be considered the most sublime of them all. [10] In a similar mood Copernicus' pupil Rheticus in his *Narratio Prima* speaks of the stars as "divine bodies". He marvels at "God's workmanship" as manifest in the symmetry of the spheres and the

---

6 *Ibid.*

7 Dagobert Frey, *Gotik und Renaissance* (Augsburg, 1929), p. 56.

8 John White, *The Birth and Rebirth of Pictorial Space* (London, s.d.), pp. 189-201.

9 *The Art of Sculpture* (Washington, 1956), p. 71.

10 *De Revolutionibus Orbium Coelestium Libri Sex* (Munich, 1949), I, 8.

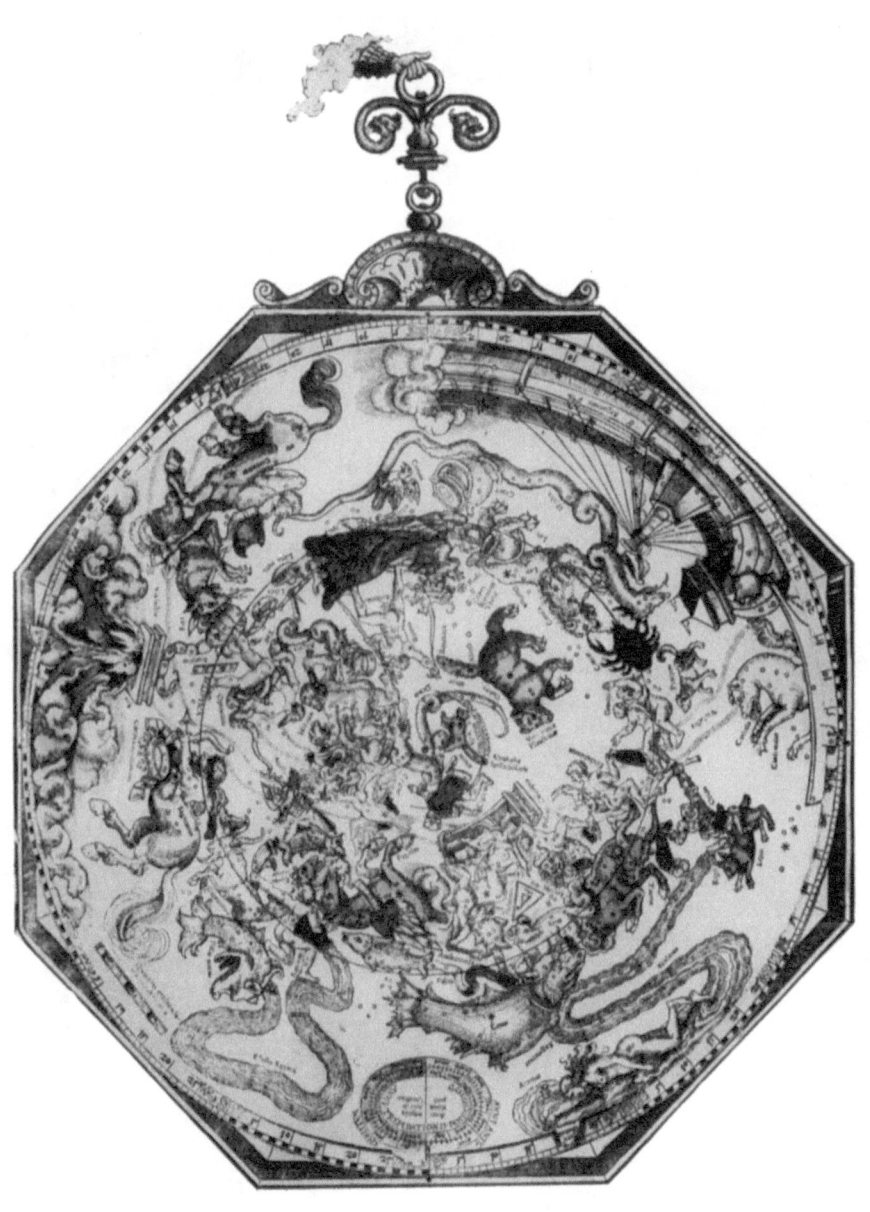

I. Apianus, *Astronomicum Caesareum*, Planisphere, 1540

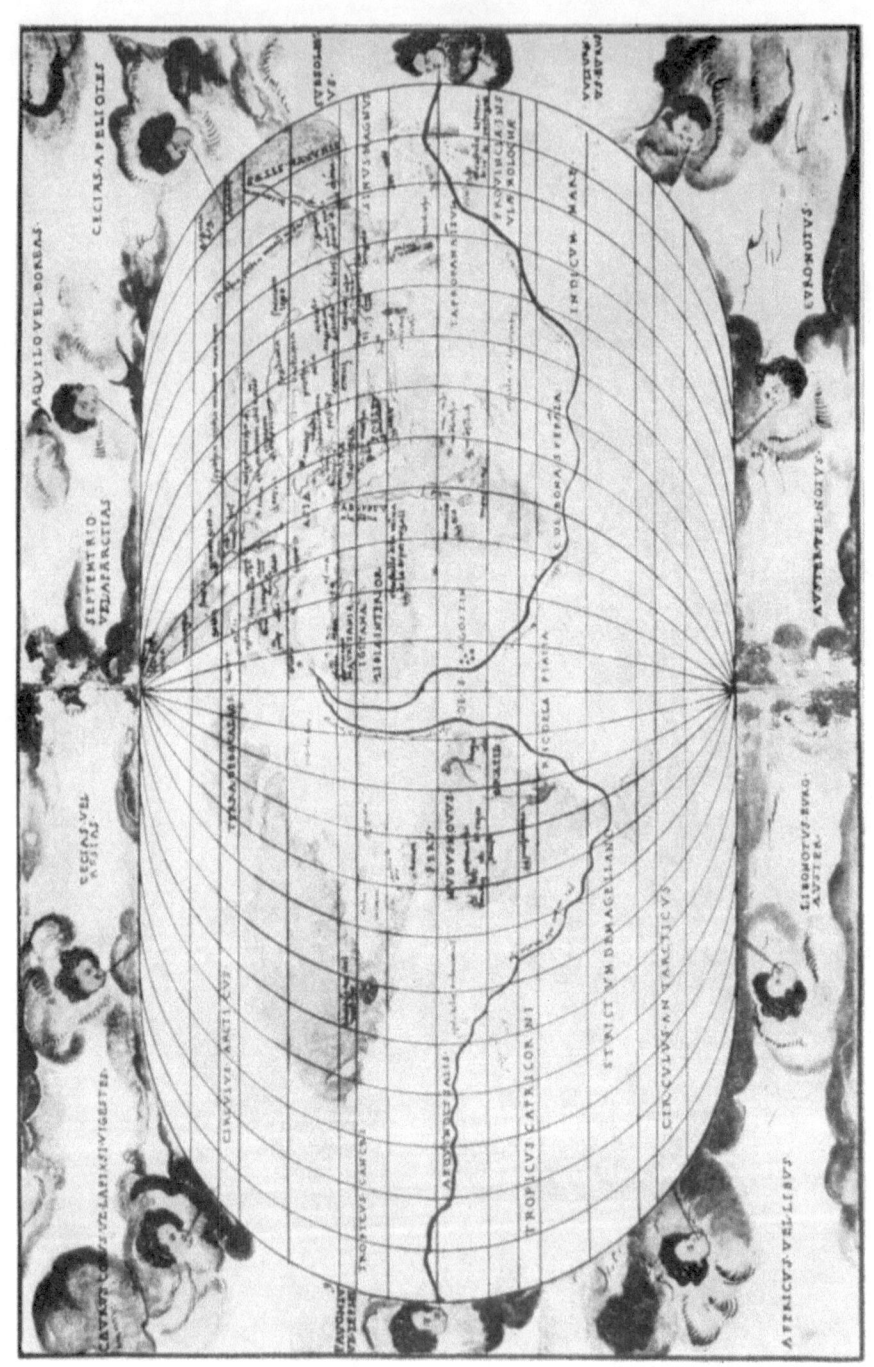

II. Battista Agnese, World Map, 1538

interconnection of their motions. [11] Tycho Brahe's *De Nova Stella*, containing the description of a star that appeared and disappeared in Cassiopeia, starts with a poetic effusion addressed to the astronomer Pratensis, that shows how moved the author was by the beatuy and brilliance of the nightly universe he kept examining in the solitude of his observatory. [12]

Characteristic also is the pictorical appeal of scientific charts and illustrations found in astronomical and geographical treatises. A Parisian edition of 1538 of Sacrobosco's *Textus de Sphera* contains a woodcut representing the "armillary sphere" that is not only a scientifically well conceived sketch, but, thanks to its geometric clarity and elegance, also a feast for the eye. [13] A planisphere in the first edition of Apianus' *Astronomicum Caesareum*, the first map of the heavens that shows with any precision the position of stars belonging to the different constellations, conveys by its plasticity and dynamic the mystery of heavy bodies moving through large empty spaces of the universe (Illustration I). [14] Lovely are some of the sixteenth century world maps, particularly those of the Venetian cartographer Battista Agnese. A map of his probably made in 1538 and having this date as its sole identification, represents the contemporary trend. (Illustration II). [15] In accordance with the then prevalent concept of the *Terra Quadripartita* [16] it contains an image of Europe, Africa, Asia and America, and even depicts the Strait of Magellan that was discovered shortly before. While geographically as correct as can be expected, this mappa mundi has unusual charm. Following a medieval tradition the earth here appears elliptical in shape (the spherical shape is prevalent in the Renaissance). [17] The seas aer white and the green of the continents and the blue of the sky are delicate and neat. At certain spots the dreamy blue of the sky darkens to show the position of the winds, concentrations of air blown towards the earth by angels of the wind. Within such a combination of shapes and colors the earth looks like

---

[11] *Three Copernican Treatises,* ed. Edward Rosen (New York, 1959), p. 145.

[12] J. L. E. Dreyer, *Tycho Brahe* (Edinburgh, 1890), p. 46.

[13] The Metropolitan Museum of Art, Dick Fund, 1914.

[14] (Ingolstadt, 1540).

[15] Fite and Freeman, *A Book of Old Maps* (Cambridge, 1926).

[16] Konrad Kretschmer, *Geschichte der Geographie* (Berlin, 1912), p. 100.

[17] Dickinson and Howarth, *The Makings of Geography* (Oxford, 1933), p. 77.

a blown-up object suspended in space. Perhaps it is an artistic interpretation of the problem that preoccupied the contemporary geogra-
pher Gerhard Kremer (Mercator) who wondered how the earth with
all its weight could be set up without a prop in the void. [18]

In the seventeenth century the artistic element tends to disappear
from scientific studies of the cosmos and the earth. Sometimes, as in
the case of Descartes's works, the visible universe disappears altogether,
giving room to pure mathematics. [19] Nor does the image of the terrestrial globe continue to stir people's imagination. With the general
recognition of the heliocentric system the suspension of the earth in
the ether becomes a theme of the past. In the publications of the
Dutchman Hondius, one of the great cartographers of the seventeenth
century, the earth as a whole has turned into a geometrical abstraction. On the other hand some pictorical interest now is focused on
life and customs in different sections of the globe, a manifestation
of the growing interest for local color. [20]

---

[18] *Gerardi Mercatoris et Hondii Atlas* (Amsterdam, 1636), p. 6. Heinrich
Averdunk, *Gerhard Mercator und die Geographen unter seinen Nachkommen*
(Gotha, 1914), pp. 86-87. The concept goes back to antiquity: "Nec circum-
fuso pendebat in aëre tellus/Ponderibus librata suis" Ovid, *Metamorphoses*
I, 12-13.

[19] Alexandre Koyré, *Entretiens sur Descartes* (New York, 1944), pp. 45-
84.

[20] *Gerardi Mercatoris et I. Hondii Atlas* (Amsterdam, 1636).

CHAPTER I

THE GROWTH OF SPACE AND VARIETY
IN FRENCH LANDSCAPES

The gradual development of the Renaissance vision of the world in France can well be observed in landscape painting. In its evolution throughout the fifteenth and sixteenth century this genre shows convincingly the growing fascination with space and variety.

Pleasure found in the observation of space is shown by the trend to give to out-of-door scenes a natural background. Previously the background was gilded or patterned, or it was altogether missing, in which case the painting was sometimes surrounded by a Gothic linear adornment. [21] The new current has been interpreted as an expression of realism. [22] It might be more to the point to speak of a growing interest in spatial representation. In the realm of religious art we are dealing with an encroachment of the temporal over the spiritual aspect of life. The solemn gold, or the geometrical ornaments behind scenes taken from the Old or New Testament or the life of the saints, convey as visual abstractions the absolute, the supernatural character of the theme. They are to make us aware of the fact that the events depicted do not essentially belong to this world. They become more emphatically part of it by the earthly setting. Such secularism is further stressed by a predilection of the artist to depict, together with the natural phenomena, characteristic images of contemporary life. It should be noted, however, that this metamorphosis

---

[21] Jehan d'Orléans, *The Altar of Narbonne*, 1374-1380, Musée National du Louvre, Paris.

[22] Dagobert Frey, *Gotik und Renaissance* (Augsburg, 1929), p. 59.

stands for a modification rather than a weakening of pious intentions. The worldly scenes now added are of a charm that seems to reflect the supernatural beauty of the central theme. [23]

The natural background appears in French paintings in the last quarter of the fourteenth century. [24] The first attempts are sparing and timid. In one of the square pieces of a shutter of an aedicula from the school of Paris painted at about 1400 and representing scenes from the life of Christ and the Holy Virgin, a hill or rock can be seen in the background and a little strip of the sky behind a flying angel who announces the birth of the Saviour to the shepherds. [25] A quadriptych from Southern France of about the same time also has a bit of natural background in the first square of the second row of the left shutter. [26] Both are outdone by a tempera from the school of Avignon from about 1390 that depicts Christ carrying the cross. [27] A castle and a mountain prominently are here displayed in the back. Interesting also is the *Nativity and Saint Christopher*, a late fourteenth century dyptich, that contains two awkwardly drawn hills. [28]

Characteristic of the evolution from the decorative to the living environment are some earlier fifteenth century illuminations. In this genre the background seems to disengage itself little by little from the branches of the initials and from the tendrils of the ornamental border. [29] Illustrative in this respect is the miniature *The Jews in Egypt* from the *Bible Historiale*. It is from about 1420. [30] (Illustration III.) The left border of his work shows an ornamental flower enclosing in its petal a biblical scene. In a double motion the trimming here turned into an organic image and then created as it were, further expressions of life within its outlines.

---

[23] Louis Cons, *Anthologie littéraire de la Renaissance française* (New York, 1945), p. XIII.

[24] John White, *The Birth and Rebirth of Pictorial Space* (London, s.d.), p. 223.

[25] School of Paris, about 1400, belongs to Charles Léon Cardon.

[26] School of Southern France, about 1400, Mr. Douglas, London.

[27] *Christ Carrying the Cross with Two Donors*, Musée National du Louvre, Paris.

[28] Musée Meyer van den Bergh, Antwerp.

[29] John White, op. cit., p. 219.

[30] Bibliothèque Nationale, Paris, Département des Manuscrits.

In the fifteenth century the background receives clarity and splendor. [31] Yet for the time being it remains limited in scope and by the general mood conveyed presents the eye of the onlooker from straying away into a distance. Its beauty now lies in its intimacy. [32] Mountains, hills and forests serve to close in the view. Together with nature the artists delight in representing castles, cities, or farm buildings that often help to set limits to the vista. They are accompanied in most cases by scenes taken from everyday life that associate with the visual effects contributing to the local character of the work. [33]

For an illustration of a still primitive treatment of the background we return once more to the above mentioned (footnote 30) miniature from the *Bible Historiale*. (Illustration III) The painting contains from the front towards the back three consecutive spatial sections, which, due to lack of experience in perspective drawing, appear practically superimposed on one another. In the foreground, two political assemblies are depicted within the walls of a slender and delicate feudal castle. [34] Behind the frontal sections, in the courtyard of the building, the Jews, supervised by their guards, are engaged in heavy physical work. In the rear of the castle appears the background itself. It shows scenes from everyday life and ends in a hill.

The planning of the work clearly reveals the trend towards spatial expansion and yet also shows the desire to close in the scene as a whole. For a representation in depth the theme itself is split into two visual units; the background, independent from the subject matter altogether, is added in an effort to create even more distance. At the same time, the atmosphere remains cozy, and thereby conforms to contemporary taste. The hill in the rear helps to restrain the view

---

[31] Not every painter has become interested in the natural background. It sometimes is omitted in subjects that call for it; e.g. *Saint Michael Felling the Dragon*, Fifteenth Century, School of Avignon.

[32] The cozy atmosphere of these landscapes is foretold by medieval representations of the earthly paradise and the *Hortus Conclusus*, both of which reach into the fifteenth century. Clark Kenneth, *Landscape into Art* (London, 1949), p. 4.

[33] Helmut A. Hatzfeld, *Literature through Art* (New York, 1952), p. 44.

[34] The custom of representing transparent walls to show scenes within the building goes back to the Italian Trecento. Jacques Lassaigne, *Flemish Painting, The Century of Van Eyck*, tr. Stuart Gilbert (Albert Skira Publishers, 1957), p. 14.

and leaves room for only a small strip of the sky. The intimacy of
the tableau is enhanced by the charming banalities found in the third
and remotest section: little houses, rooftops, a windmill, a horseman,
dogs, people engaged in agricultural work etc.

More elegant and better drawn is the *Altar-screen of the Parliament of Paris* that dates from the middle of the fifteenth century. [35]
(Illustration IV) It is a crucifixion with Saint John and the Virgin
standing under the cross, surrounded at some distance by four historical or holy individuals, two on each side: Saint Louis and Saint
John the Baptist to the left and Saint Denis and Charlemagne to the
right. The work has been called "Gothic" and "awkward" by Gillet [36]
and is, nevertheless, exquisite as regards its treatment of the background. It contains a landscape, three faithhfully depicted passages
of the city of Paris and scenes of everyday living. The intimacy
created by territorial elevations is heightened by the particularly affectionate presentation of the city and its life. The work reminds in this
respect of contemporary Flemish paintings. [37]

The desire to evoke distance and yet also restrain it, here materializes in masterfully conceived and contradictory artistic schemes.
The city of Paris in the back is unobtrusive in line and color. It is
dreamy and remote like an afterthought. At the same time it is thematically blended with the foreground and thereby close to the spectator. As our eyes wander from the front towards the back we are
never quite sure where the biblical scene ends and where Paris starts.
At some distance behind the cross, on a hill that may be Golgotha
or the *Montagne Sainte-Geneviève* stands the traditional group of
Roman soldiers. A tittle further back some individuals are engaged in
conversation that may or may not refer to the biblical event. Way
in the back, on the left hand side of the painting that reproduces the
Ile de la Cité, a few idling men can be seen on the left bank of
the Seine. One of them, leaning over a barrier, looks into the water.

The intimate landscape as defined above reaches its climax in the
calendar section of the *Très riches heures du Duc de Berry* by
the Franco-Flemish Limbourg Brothers. [38] Although the work belongs

---

[35] Muséa National du Louvre, Paris.
[36] Louis Gillet, *Les primitifs français* (Marseille, 1941), p. 41.
[37] *Ibid.*, 56-57. Jacques Dupont, *Les primitifs français* (Paris, s.d.), p. 37.
[38] Musée Condé, Chantilly.

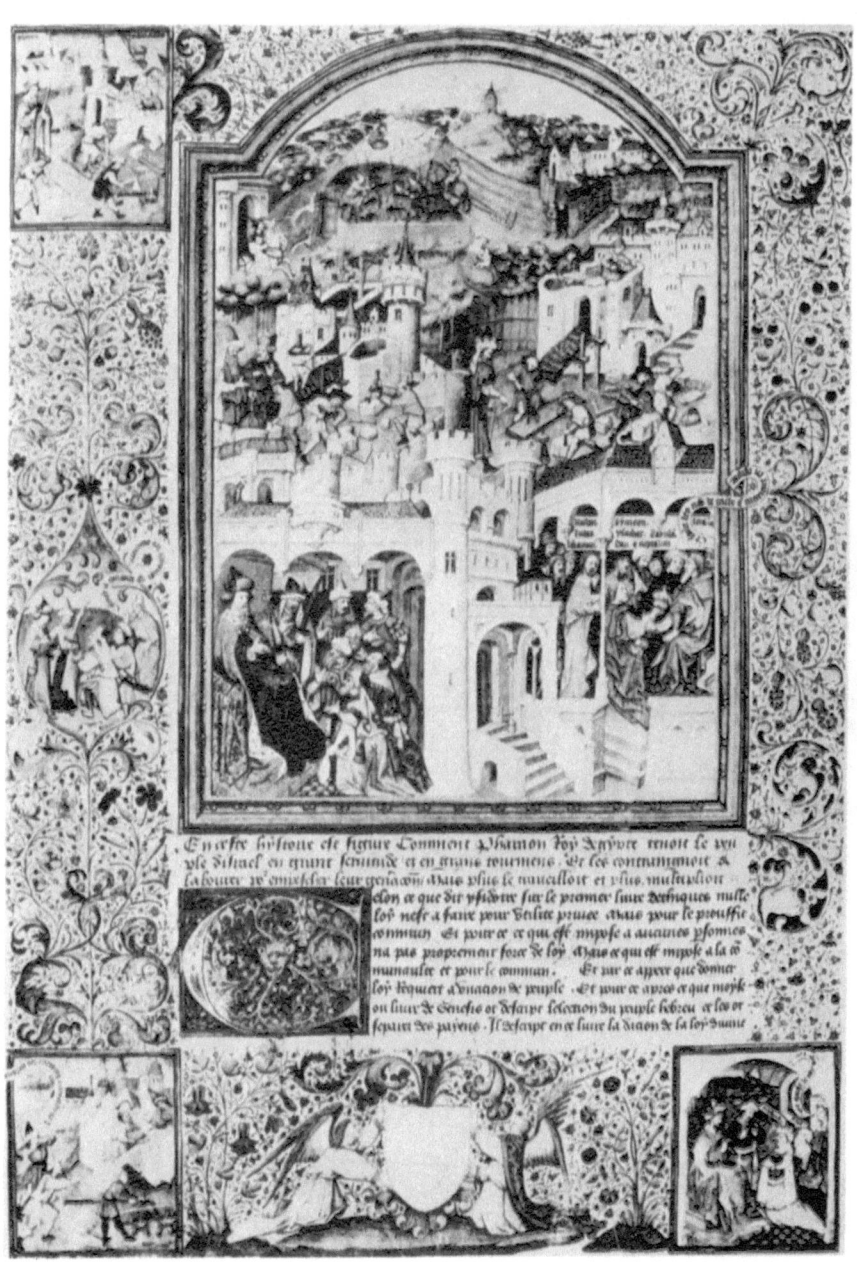

III. *Bible Historiale, The Jews in Egypt.* About 1420, Bibliothèque
Nationale, Paris

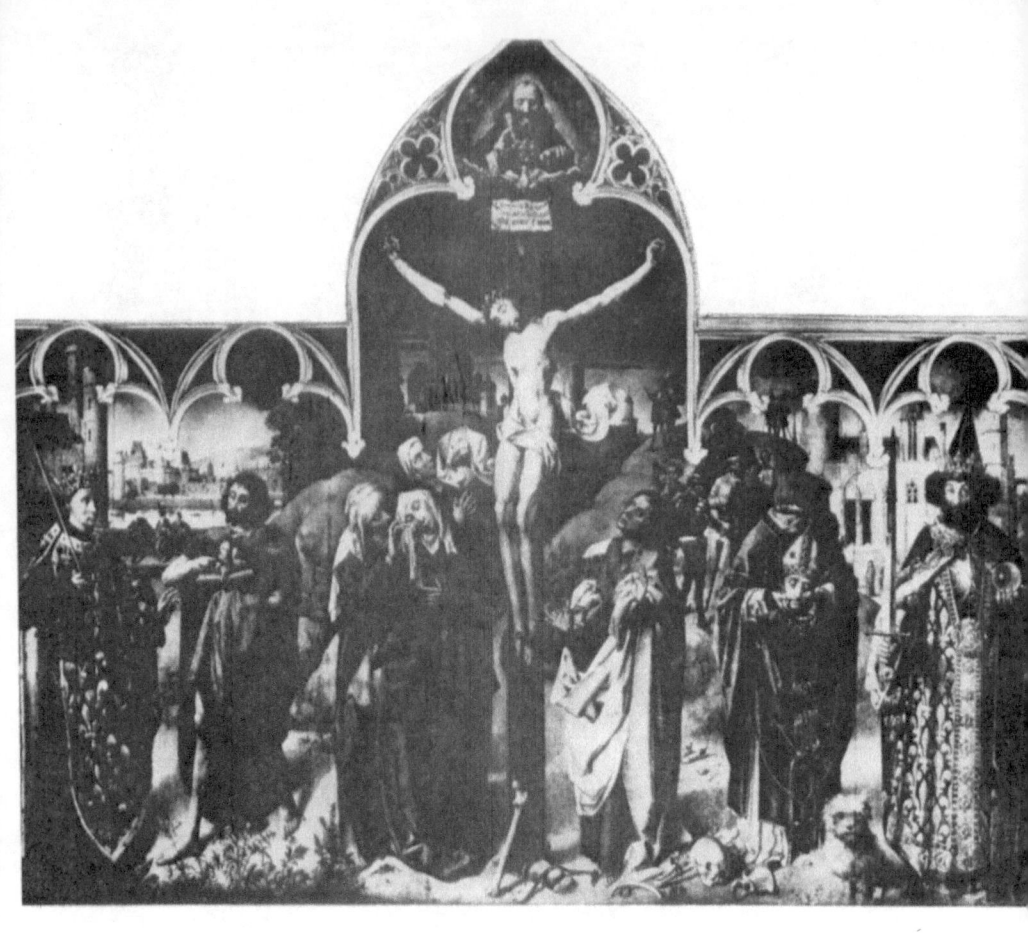

IV. *Altar-screen of the Parliament of Paris.* About 1450, Musée National
du Louvre, Paris

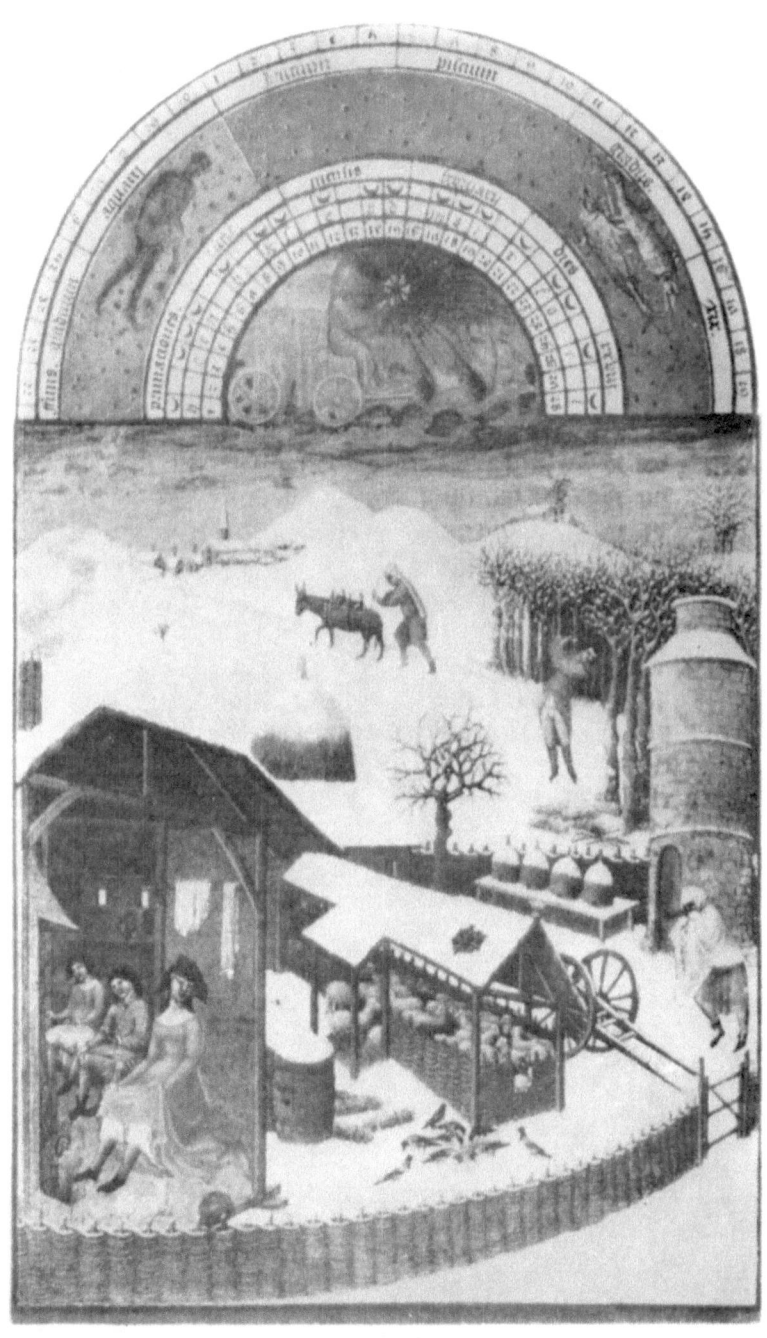

V. *Les très riches heures du Duc de Berry, Le mois de février*, 1418 or 1419,
Musée Condé, Chantilly

to the early part of the century (1418 or 1419) and precedes the paintings here previously discussed, we left it because of its superiority to the last. For these excellent painters developed the landscape to a level, that far from being reached by their contemporaries, destined them to become the unsurpassed model of a number of masters of the second part of the century. [39]

The eleven landscapes of this series depict the occupations of the months and are of a warmth, a delicacy, a refinement and a splendor that fill the eye with wonder and delight. For a backdrop the artists here use not only hills and mountains but also forests [40] and in most cases rather prominent buildings, placed either in the middle or going from one end of the scene to the other. [41] These buildings not only help to bar the view, but they add very effectively to the familiarity of the atmosphere. In some ways they are unearthly and seem to belong in their slender beauty to the world of fairytales. Yet they also emanate contemporary truth and residential warmth. The majority are identified as fifteenth century castles or cities that belong to the duke or were visible from his feudal properties. In front of them peasants can be seen performing agricultural work or ladies or gentlemen engaged in lordly entertainments. Each scenery is a little earthly paradise that sets the imagination at rest and stops it from wanting to go beyond the limits of the scene presented.

Highly illustrative for our purpose, although sligthly different from the rest, is the *Month of February* (Illustration V) that shows a snowcovered country scene of great charm. Little of the sky can be seen and the wintry clouds that cover it contribute to the general mood of enclosedness. Instead of feudal castles as found in the rest of the miniatures we here have a remote village on top of a hill that shuts out the view. Intimacy in this case spreads from the foreground to the rest of the composition: in a farm house three individuals, a peasant woman, her male servant and her maid warm themselves at a fireplace. [42] The mood seems to radiatae from inside the building

---

[39] Gillet, op. cit., p. 22.

[40] *The Month of May, The Month of December.*

[41] *The Month of June, The Month of September, The Month of October.*

[42] Helmut Hatzfeld, "The Discovery of Realistic Art in Antoine de la Sale through Pol de Limbourg," *Modern Language Quarterly*, XV, 2 (June, 1954), p. 170.

into the exterior world. The farmyard shows a flock of sheep comfortably crowding against each other in their fold. A freezing peasant rushes towards the barn, another one cuts a tree, undoubtedly to provide firewood. And a man who drives his mule along the hillside towards the village seems to be hurrying to his own warm home.

In the *Month of May* (Illustration VI) the artist brings about similar effects in a sunlit landscape. Here too the sky is de-emphasized. In the absence of hills a thick forest with rooftops standing out from behind it, forms a highly protective background. The ducal holdings here represented is Riom, the capital of the duchy of Auvergne, a fief of the duke. The cavalcade in the foreground commemorates a spring festival held every May first at the ducal court. By dint of its private character it fills the protected spot with friendliness. On the *Month of April* perhaps the loveliest of them all, an engagement between a young nobleman and noblewoman can be seen in a garden before the castle of Orge. The *Month of August* shows a group of gentlemen and ladies engaged in falcon hunting at the castle of Etampes.

Among numerous paintings that here could be mentioned as examples, some stress nature more than buildings as a background and vice versa. *The Temptation of Saint Anthony* from Simon Marmion's *Book of Hours* presents a deeply secluded spot within a forest with only a barn as a fabric. [43] Jean Fouquet's *Saint Marguerite as a Shepherdess* from the *Hours of Etienne Chevalier* [44] the natural scenery is far less prominent, yet occupies two thirds of the background. The contrary can be said of the *Entry of Emperor Charles IV. in the Abbey of Saint Denis* (Illustration VII), a miniature made on a drawing of Jean Fouquet that shows in a small opening between prominent buildings a hill and a river. [45] Some paintings from Provence have a stony atmosphere and a certain number among them, like the *Adoration of the Child Jesus* from the school of Provence [46] and the *Pietà of Villeneuve-les-Avignon* [47] are almost pure architecture. In some cases the harsh impression caused by the absence or

[43] 1459, British Museum, London.
[44] 1452-1460. Musée National du Louvre, Paris.
[45] *Les grandes chroniques,* about 1460. Bibliothèque Nationale, Paris.
[46] About 1480, Musée Calvet, Avignon.
[47] Fifteenth Century, Musée National du Louvre, Paris.

neglect of nature is made up for by the beauty and brilliance of structures. The *Pietà and Donor of the School of Avignon* [48] produces with two bare mountains two sparkling Gothic churches in the background. In some cases nature and stone, both prominent, form a whole, giving life and charm to each other. In Fouquet's *Saint Anne and the Three Marys* [49] the garden and the city flow together creating a harmonious background.

A number of interesting paintings in which the city prevails as a background, offer through street perspectives a tantalising effect of both spatial penetration and spatial limitation. The receding flight of houses gives an insinuating illusion of increase and also of diminution. Characteristic in this respect is the *Miracle of Saint Mitre* painted by a member of the school of Nicolas Froment. [50] The affectionate presentation of street scenes often makes such a scene peculiarly attractive. Admirable are the dainty and tidy houses along the street lines that appear behind the open doors or windows of some of the interiors of the Master of Flemalle. [51] The scenes are probably influenced by paintings of commercially highly developed Flanders. [52]

The far deeper penetration of space that takes place in the French sixteenth century changes the character of the landscape altogether. The atmosphere tends to become cosmic, and the pleasure felt formerly at the familiarity of the view now is replaced by the artist's marveling at the magnitude of the world. The vertical backdrop diminishes or disappears, permitting the eye to move into distance. The sky becomes more prominent, and hills and mountains appear to be incidental elevations within far reaching vistas. Flying and

---

[48] 1470-1480, The Frick Collection, New York.

[49] The *Hours of Etienne Chevalier*, 1452-1460, Bibliothèque Nationale, Paris.

[50] v. also Jean Fouquet, *The Building of the Temple, Antiquités judaïques*, approximately 1470-1476, Bibliothèque Nationale, Paris; Jean Fouquet or his studio, *The Coronation of King Louis VI., Les grandes chroniques de France*, Bibliothèque Nationale, Paris; Master of Saint Sebastian, *Saint Sebastian interceding for the Plague-Stricken*, Panel from the *Altarpiece of Saint Sebastian*, Walters Art Galery, Baltimore.

[51] The *Mérode Altarpiece, Virgin and Child*, third decade of the fifteenth century, The Cloisters, New York.

[52] Jan van Eyck, *The Madonne of Chancellor Rollin*, about 1425, Musée National du Louvre; *Virgin and Child with Saints and Donor*, 1435-1436, Musée National de Louvre, Paris. Baron Joseph van der Elst, *The Last Flowering of the Middle Ages* (Garden City, New York, 1945).

hovering objects, a favorite theme of the period, often are depicted to give us a feel of the immensity of aerial expanse. Buildings become vague in drawing and color; in some cases they appear fantastic, work on our imagination, and thereby help our eyes to escape. Manifestations of daily living, while at times still depicted lose their former warmth and no longer localize the subject matter. Often their effect is blurred by mythological scenes that by now tend to become the very topic of the painting. Thus the landscape strays away from the contemporary mood not only in space but also in time. The Renaissance ideal now is complete: both the visual and the historical barriers are gone.

Whereas some signs of the coming manner can be detected in the latter part of the fifteenth century, particularly in certain paintings of the Master of Moulins,[53] of Nicolas Froment[54] and Jean Bourdichon[55] the movement reaches its climax in the sixteenth century, most clearly in the School of Fontainebleau. Although the Italian mannerists who create this school, manifest the Renaissance of their own country in a state of change, they help to spread the Renaissance in their new environment. Their spatial vision has been considered unrealistic because they followed their imagination rather than any natural model[56] and dreamt their scenery into the infinite.[57] Perhaps the strenuous search for realism, a favorite concept of positivistic critics, prevents us from finding the innate values of artistic and literary movements. The works of the so-called mannerists are magnificent as well as true. They teach the French artists to look at the world with visual freedom and to roam in space.

Characteristic of the new movement are Niccolo dell'Abate's *Eurydice* and *Aristarchus*[58] and his *Abduction of Proserpine*.[59] (Illustration VIII) In both cases an extensive piece of land flows together with a cloudy sky that leads the vistas in the artist's interpretation towards further spaces unknown, towards the universe. In the first

---

[53] *Portrait of a Young Princess*, Collection Robert Lehmann, New York.
[54] *The Burning Bush*, 1475-1476, Cathedral of Aix.
[55] *Virgin and Child*, 1491, National Museum of Naples.
[56] Lionello Venturi, *The Sixteenth Century*, tr. Stuart Gilbert (Editions d'art Albert Skira, 1956), p. 229.
[57] Silvia Béguin, *L'école de Fontainebleau* (Paris, 1960), pp. 229-230.
[58] About 1558-1560, Lancaster House, London.
[59] About 1558-1560, Musée National du Louvre, Paris.

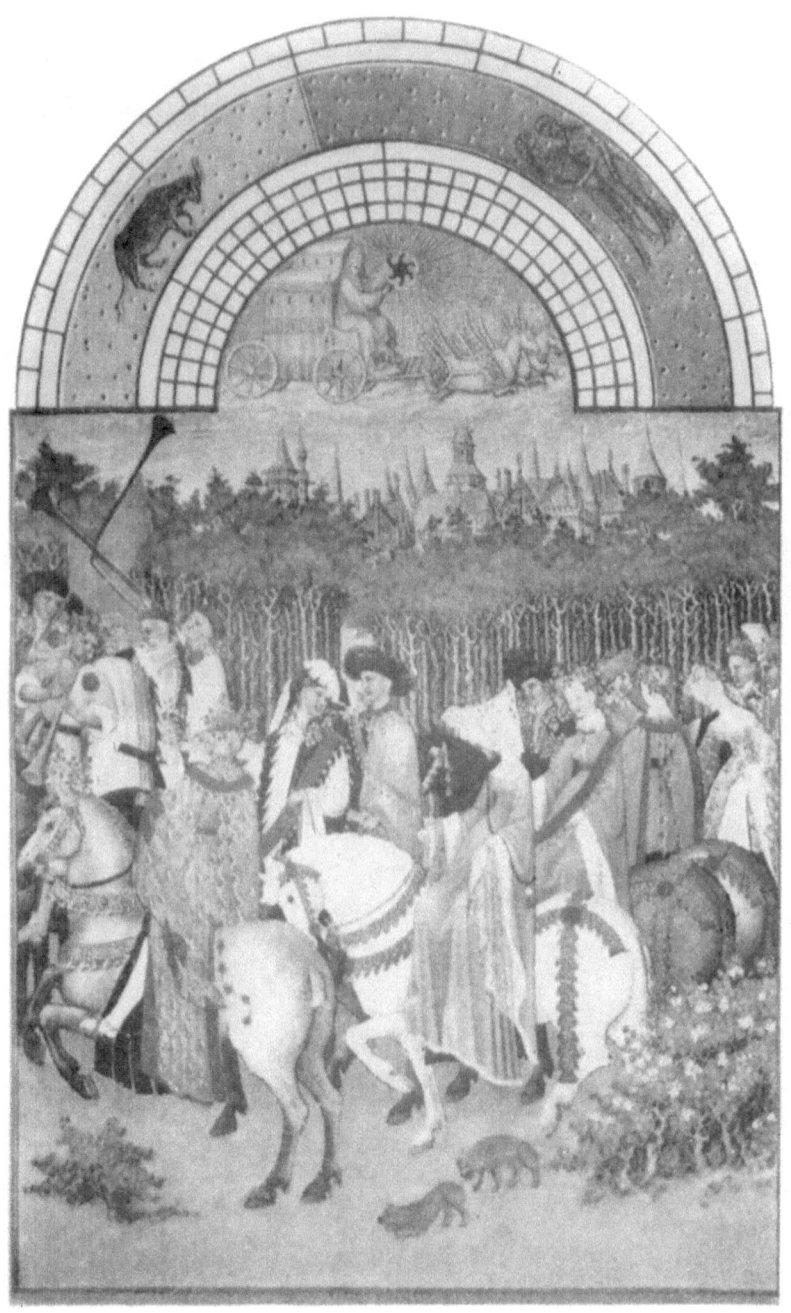

VI. *Les très riches heures du Duc de Berry, Le mois de mai,* 1418 or 1419,
Musée Condé, Chantilly

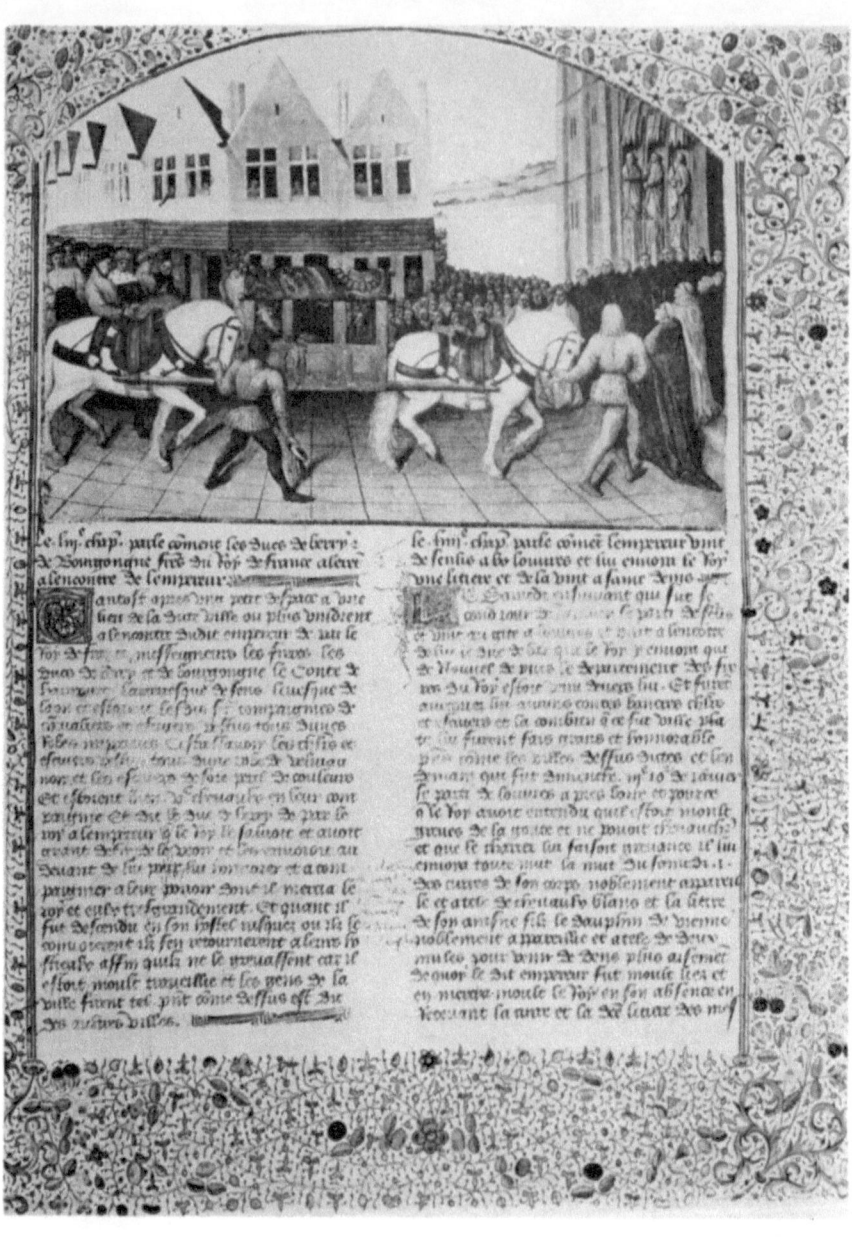

VII. *Entry of Charles IV. in the Abbey of Saint Denis, Les Grandes Chroniques*, about 1460, Bibliothèque Nationale, Paris

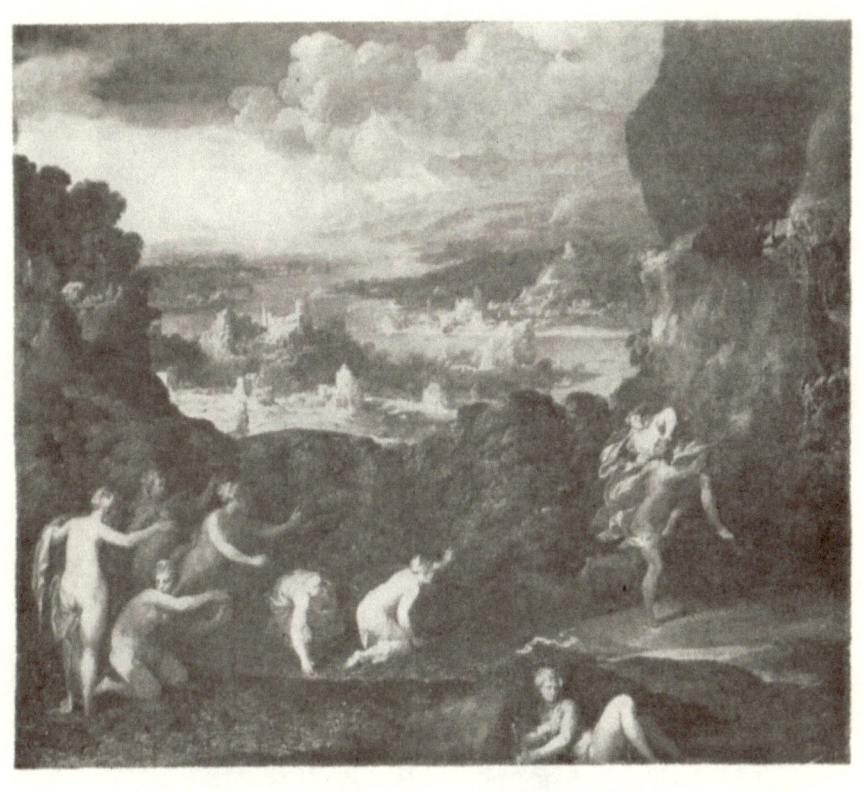

VIII. Niccolò dell'Abbate, *Abduction of Proserpine*. About 1558-1560,
Musée National du Louvre, Paris

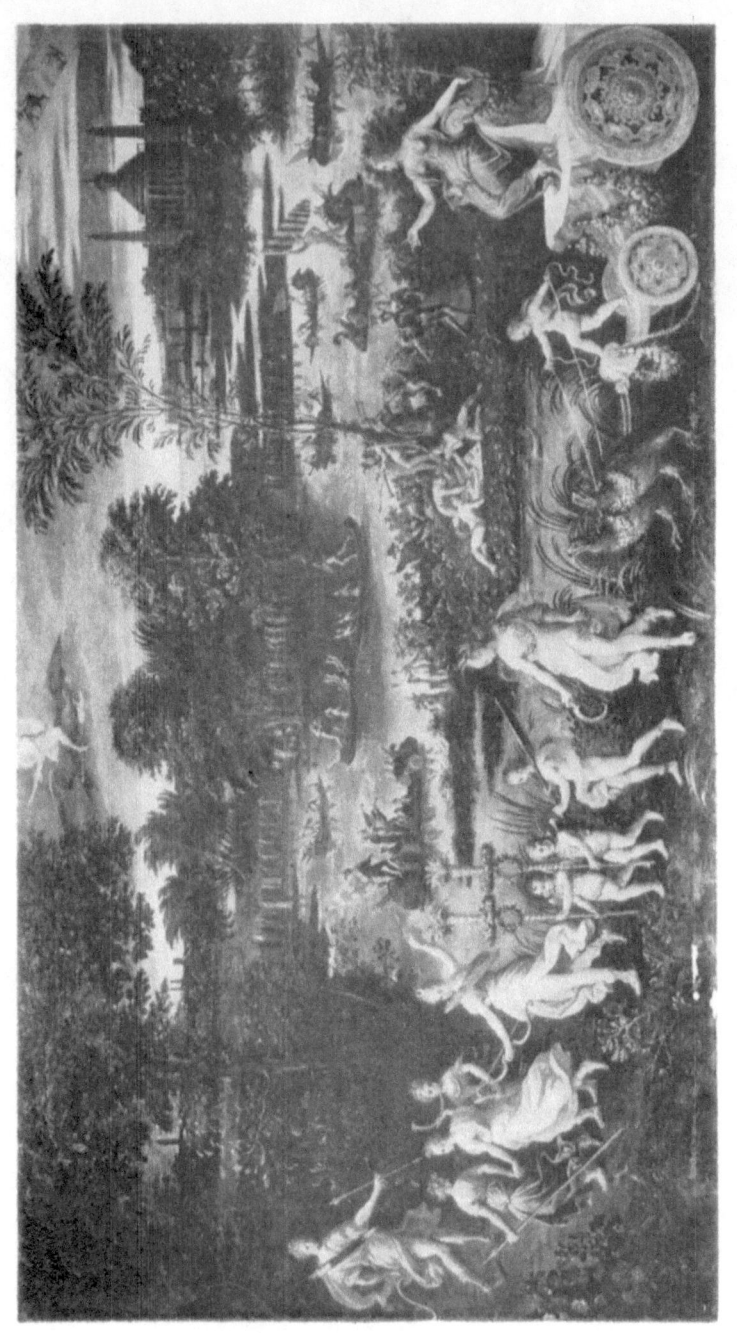

IX. Antoine Caron, *Triumph of the Summer*. About 1570, Wildenstein Gallery, New York

of the two paintings a large body of water contributes to the cosmic atmosphere. In the second a winding river leads our eyes to the back and disappears in the clouded sky. The hills and mountains in these works, big as they may be if considered by themselves appear as slight elevations in the horizontally unfolding view. As for the cities and castles that can be seen in the background, they are vague and elusive and seem to belong to an enchanted world. They are in harmony with the mythological scenes in the foreground, and link up with them to interpret the fantastic size of the landscape.

Interesting for our analysis is Caron's *Triumph of the Summer.* [60] (Illustration IX) because it reproduces a festivity at court, a theme that would call for a familiar atmosphere and yet moves out into space. Although there are trees in the background, they do not create an impression of enclosedness. Dense as they are in the center, they become more scattered on the left of the painting and unsubstantial towards the right. The body of water in front of the trees escapes at a certain point towards the back, removing what little intimacy may have been left. At its farthest visible point it is crossed by a bridge: this makes us think of more water, and, thereby, of more spaces to come. The image of Jupiter flying on a tremendous eagle towards signs of the Zodiac marked on the sky, link the scene to mythological and astronomical concepts of the universe.

These principles do not materialize in all landscapes fully or with the same effect. A number of out-of-door scenes are completely enclosed, some for contrast in colors, as is the case in the *Angelica and Medor* of a painter from the circle Toussaint Debreuil's [61] or because the subject matter requires it altogether. The very tale demands to place into a forest the feminine nudes of *Diana's Bath*, a work copied from François Clouet [62] and of the *Allegory* of an unknown painter. [63] Characteristically though the absence of any contemporary civilization and something unusual or even sinister in the natural surroundings of these works give us a feeling of the remote and thereby fall in with the mythological subject matter. At other times a slight opening

---

[60] About 1570. Wildenstein Gallery, New York.
[61] Early seventeenth century, Musée National du Louvre, Paris. Beginnings of the dramatic frame of mind of the baroque here are felt.
[62] About 1550-1560, Musée des Beaux Arts, Rouen.
[63] About 1570-1580, Musée National du Louvre, Paris.

found next to a prominent natural barrier suffices to show distance. [64]
Often a feeling of intimacy that may be caused by a mountain set up
rather conspicuously in the rear is effectively counteracted by the
fantastic aspects of the landscape. [65] Settings of this kind sometimes
are more effective in creating a feeling of remoteness than wide open
spaces.

Prominently displayed perspectives in town scenes also have
become more voluminous. They now convey an impression of unlimited space while the static quality of the city has disappeared. This
can be well observed in certain works of Caron. In his *Emperor
Augustus and the Sibyl of Tibur* [66] the receding street line becomes
gradually less distinctive and seems to evaporate in the distance. In
the *Massacre of the Triumvirs* [67] a flight of houses leads towards distant mountains in whose presence the urbane milieu can hardly prevail.
And in the *Astronomers* that shows an eclipse of the sun, the street
seems to move into the cosmos. [68]

In certain paintings depicting country life brisk or even exaggerated
motion help to disrupt the static quality that easily associates with
such a theme. The animated and almost frantically toiling agricultural
laborers in the foreground of Giulio Camillo's *Landscape with Thresh-
ers* [69] differ essentially from the sedate peasants of the Limbourg
Brothers. They fit the large and airy landscape in the back.

Sometimes motion brings even into protected areas a suggestion
of broad spaces. Very effective in such cases is the introduction of
flight. In the famous *Triumph of Flora* of an unknown master of the
School of Fontainebleau that shows the goddess seated in front of a
tree with abundant foliage, a number of flying cupids bring into the

---

[64] Luca Penni, *Diana Hunting*, about 1550, Musée National du Louvre,
Paris.

[65] Jean Cousin (attributed to) *Charity*, about 1543, Musée Fabre, Montpellier; Dumoustier (?) *Profetess Anna Consecrating her Son Samuel*, Miniature from the *Book of Hours of the Connétable de Montmorency*, 1549,
Musée Condé, Chantilly; School of Rosso, *Story of Esau*, about 1540,
fresco, Château d'Ecouen.

[66] About 1580, Musée National du Louvre, Paris.

[67] About 1562, Musée de Beauvais.

[68] About 1571, Collection Sir Anthony Blunt, London.

[69] About 1560-1565, Château de Fontainebleau, same painter, *The Reap-
ers*, about 1560-1565, Collection Riechers, Paris.

sheltered milieu the fresh air of the wide open spaces. [70] (Illustration X.)

Variety, the second point of our analysis, goes hand in hand with the development of space and increases from the fifteenth to the sixteenth century. It must be discussed in its relation to multitudinousness with which it associates naturally, since both are a manifestation of a passion for abundance. Let us observe that infatuation with multitudes is strongly developed in the late Middle Ages and does not increase with the coming of the Renaissance. Yet it improves its visual effect by the growth of variety in the sixteenth century. Individually discernible objects within a crowd, convey numerousness more convincigly than similar ones, for the latter create in their final effect an impression of homogeneity. In some of its finest works the Renaissance rids itself of agglomeration altogether and conveys through variety, manifest within a few items, an impression of abundance.

Some fifteenth century primitives paint crowds formed of individuals that cannot be distinguished from one another. In the right tablet of the dyptich *King Richard II. at the Feet of the Virgin Mary* a group of identical angels form a chorus. [71] They can most easily be counted by their long and delicate wings that stand out in parallel formations above them. They express the piety of the artist. Why should angels differ from one another? Similar is the impression made by the *Altar of Narbone* by a detachment of soldiers that stand at the foot of the cross behind each other and most of whom can be discerned only by their helmets. [72]

Diversity within masses makes itself felt to some extent in the fifteenth century. The *Entry of Emperor Charles IV. in the Abbey of Saint Denis* (Illustration VII., *v.* footnote 45) shows large crowds of people in several postures and positions. They face different directions or are placed on different levels. Those following the emperor in the procession walk from left to right and face an assemblage of monks who expect the visitor in front of the church. In the background a tremendous number of spectators stand *en face*. And as if still not satisfied with either the number or the variety of the spectacle, the

---

[70] About 1560, Collection Count Giuseppe Canera di Salasco, Vicenza.

[71] Anonymous, 1396, belongs to Lord Pembroke.

[72] *v.* footnote 21.

painter produced some more individuals in the second floor windows of a building in the back.

Incomparably more refined is the feeling for masses and the sense of diversity of the Limbourg Brothers. In the *Month of May* (Illustration VI., *v.* footnote 38) it is not so much the number of noblemen and noblewomen and musicians and horses, but the closeness and density of these figures that produces an illusion of multitude. Within the group variety materializes by differences in the movement of the horses, and of the direction in which the persons forming the procession turn their heads or their bodies. The musicians too stand in various postures which are made spectacular by the musical instruments they are holding.

Sometimes magnitude and variety materialize at different spots of the same composition. In the twice mentioned miniature *The Jews in Egypt* (Illustration IV., *v.* footnote 30) the members of the two assemblies seen in the foreground are huddled together in a tight cluster. Variety appears on the second plane among the more dispersed figures of the Jews. They differ from one another in their performance, their motions, their positions. Some cut stones, some do woodwork, some build a tower; some are on the ground and some are on top of a wall. The people depicted on the third plane add to the image a further touch of diversity in their relation to the theme as a whole and to one another. Extraneous as they are to the biblical facts in question, they serve to add to the events depicted still another circumstance of life. Within their own domain they form a motley group of people. An individual entering on horseback through a gate from the left seems to return from hunting. In a field some workers are engaged in agricultural tasks. To the right women seem to be making conversation and running dogs further animate the scene. Enjoyable is the rhythm between multitudinousness and multifariousness in the *Month of February* of the Limbourg Brothers (Illustration V., *v.* footnote 38). The animals pressed together in the sheepfold form a solid mass. Dispersed around them are beehives, barrels, a dovecote, a haystack, a pushcart and magpies that feed on the ground and also create diversity among themselves by their motions.

Yet nothing in the French fifteenth century can be compared to the dazzling variety of the French Renaissance. While just as fascinat-

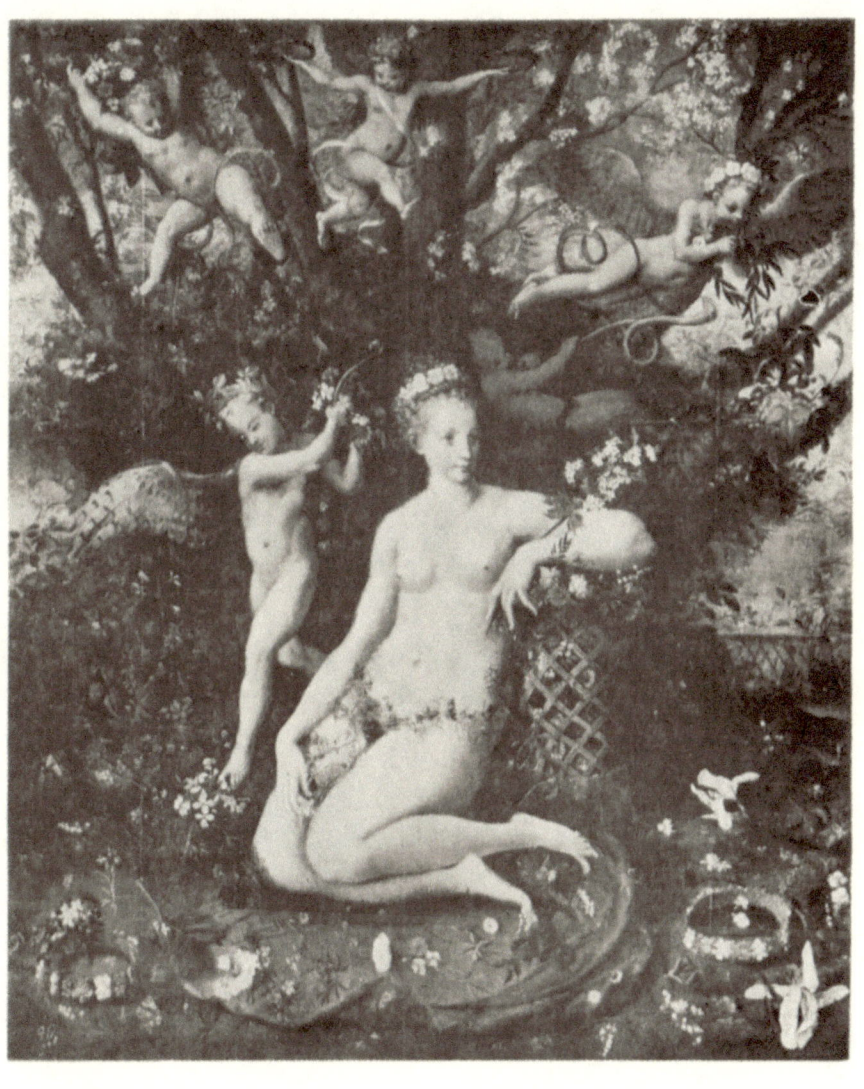

X. *Triumph of Flora*, about 1560, Collection Count Guiseppe Canera di Salasco, Vicenza

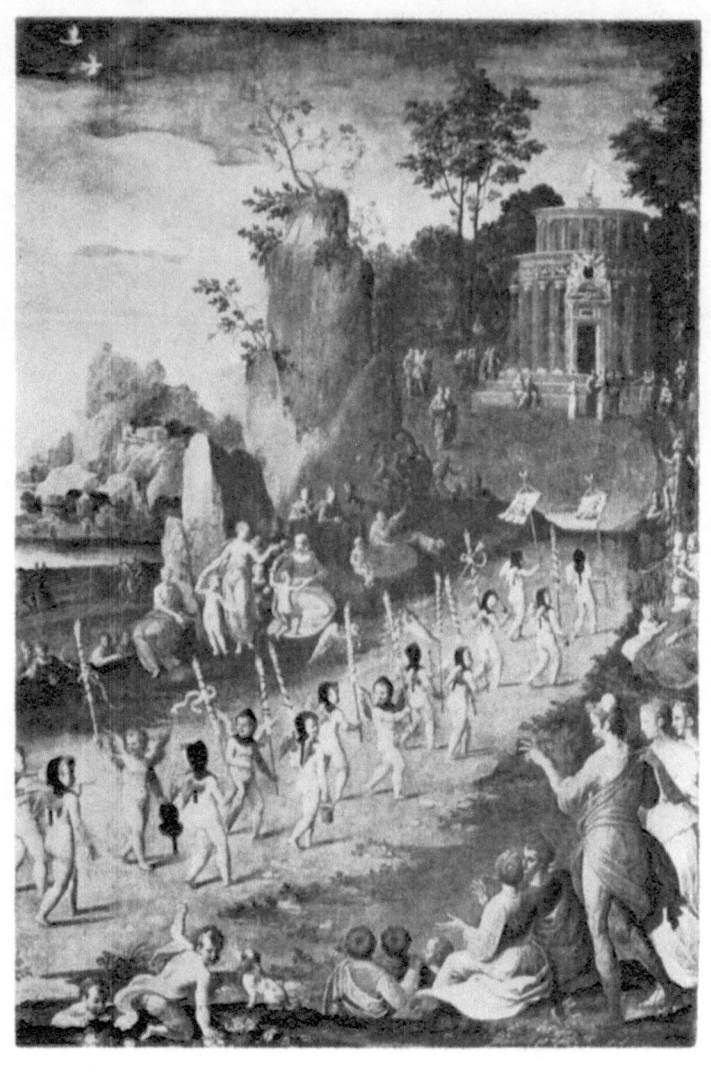

XI. *Funeral of Love*. About 1562, Musée National du Louvre, Paris

ed by masses, the latter presents only occasionally homogeneous groups within a composition; the artist now takes delight in producing figures and motives that counteract and complement, beautify and exult one another in a kaleidoscopic whole.

Caron in his *Triumph of the Summer* (Illustration IX., *v.* footnote 60) presents with diversity the multitudes he depicted by the mingling of three unrelated visual media as well as by differences in the exterior and motion of single objects. Authentic realities of sixteenth century life here are fused with mythology and a dreamworld of the painter's invention. In the most distant part of the tableau a large group of spectators are watching a water joust, probably the reproduction of an entertainment organized at the court of the Valois that seems, as already mentioned, to be the basis of the theme as a whole. The opposite shore of the river shows a paradisiac image with possibly antique reminiscences, in which naked men and women feast and move about freely in the view of all. In the foreground a pageantry of antique gods and goddesses can be seen, that may also go back to an item on the program of the royal divertissement. However it does not present itself as a masquerade but as a genuine gathering of Olympic divinities.

With the exception of the spectators that can hardly be distinguished from one another and form a cluster in the rear, every part of the painting offers great variety within its own limits. The eight boats on the water differ in size, shape and motion. Among the revelers some are naked and some are dressed, some eat, some dance, some play musical instruments, some converse and some swim or are getting ready for swimming. The diversity of the front section derives from its symbolism and from the movement of the figures that form the parade. Apollo leads the way, bow and arrow in hand. He is followed by the three feminine hunting companions of Diana, one of whom holds a spear, while another one blows a horn. Behind them walks Diana herself with a bow and arrow. Two cupids carry flowering trophies. Behind them marches an adolescent with a tree branch on his shoulder. Then comes Ceres a sickle in her hand, and finally a chariot pulled by two eagles, driven by amor and having on its platform a feminine figure that represents the summer. In its symbolic effect the procession evokes the richness of the seasons in beauty and in pleasures: the bright sunlight, the estival moon, hunting and lovemaking and flowers and thees and the harvest. With regard to motion the group is animated by a motive frequently found in Renaissance paintings, the whimsical turning of heads and bodies in various directions. Apollo, one of the huntresses, one of the cupids and one of the eagles look backward. Two of the huntresses are holding hands and look at each other, and Diana looks right out of the painting.

In this respect the work reminds of a procession of cupids in the *Funeral of Love* made by a painter of the circle of Caron. [73] (Illustration XI.) While all alike in their exterior and outfit, the little marchers enliven the image by their intercommunication and their gestures. Except for the first two and the last two each one turns his head or body towards another member of the group, or towards the people assembled around them who respond with gestures of their own. The motions are never quite the same. Four cupids turn back to look at those behind them, one over his right, another over his left shoulder, a third turns back halfway, a fourth almost completely. One of them looks to the left and five to the right, and each of the last five in a different angle and with a slightly different posture.

In some paintings variety reaches a new climax even among French Renaissance works. The *Massacre of the Triumvirate* [74] by Caron shows a Roman street filled with innumerable soldiers who pursue, kill and cut off the heads of their victims with a diversity of movements that practically defies analysis. In the background, around the doors and windows of the houses, more people participate in the general commotion and some individuals jump from the top of burning houses into the streets. An old man who in the midst of the carnage sleeps in a cave, adds by contrast another touch of variety to the theme.

In many ways the greater variety of the sixteenth century is indicative and harmoniously adjusted to spatial expansion. For in its most typical form variety goes hand in hand with dispersion and dispersion points towards larger volumes. As we approach the Renaissance, the dense masses of people the fifteenth century often liked to represent, tend to scatter. A comparison between the processions in

---

[73] About 1562, Musée National du Louvre, Paris.

[74] 1572; also: Caron, *Massacre of the Triumvirs*, about 1562, Musée de Beauvais, Beauvais.

the *Entry of Emperor Charles IV. in the Abbey of Saint Denis* (Illustration VII., *v.* footnote 45) and in the *Funeral of Love*. (Illustration XI., *v.* footnote 73) readily show this evolution that could be studied in numerous examples. [75]

Some artists being endowed with a fine feel for balance have expressed by the rhythm and the succession of the movements of individuals the relationship between variety and space. In the *Month of May* of the Limbourg Brothers (Illustration VI., footnote 38) whose beauty is dependent on spatial limitation, shows a thickly set crowd of horsemen and musicians whose various bodily movements point inward. The first two horsemen look back towards the middle of the assemblage and the two most spectacular trumpeters stand on both sides of the band, closing the group sidewise by the direction in which they are standing and upwards by their instruments that cross each other. [73] But in Niccolò dell'Abbate's *Eurydice and Aristarchus* or his *Abduction of Proserpine* (Illustration VII., *v.* footnote 59) the individuals in the foreground point in the rhythmic relation of their movements towards outer space. In the latter painting six feminine figures on the left gesture in a diversity of ways, their bodies bent increasingly forward, from left to right towards the running figure of Pluto. One of the women who seems to gather flowers and another placed in a cave towards the right, add a touch of placidity to the scene without interfering noticeably with its dynamics. Let us finally mention once more the *Triumph of Flora* (Illustration X., *v.* footnote 70) certainly one of the most beautiful works of the French Renaissance. We have mentioned briefly that the enclosed milieu of this work turns airy thanks to the presence of flying cupids. It should be added now that by the varied pattern of their motions these figures intimate that they come from space and return to it. The one on the top left seems to have dropped from above, the second, taking over the cadence, flutters towards the right. The third one descends, hovering on the right hand side of the painting. Here too one of the figures

---

[75] *v.* for closely knit crowds in medieval paintings Simon Marmion, *Altar-screen of Saint Bertin*, Deutsches Museum, Berlin, and Jean Fouquet, *Reception of a Message by François de Rochechouart*, miniature from the *Antiquités Judaïques*, approximately 1470-1476, Bibliothèque Nationale, Paris.

interferes slightly, for the sake of more diversity, with the general trend. He lies in the foliage and rests. Yet by the direction in which he lies he links up with the fifth one who runs away on the left side bottom. With an economy of means this excellent artist has evoked multitude and richness and variety and space.

CHAPTER II

THE GROWTH OF SPACE AND VARIETY
IN FRENCH LITERATURE

LEMAIRE DE BELGES

1. LEMAIRE AND THE PAINTERS

To move from painting to literary imagery is a tantalizing experience. Leonardo da Vinci well defined the difference between the two by calling literature a blind painting. [76] To me, the historian, pictorial art is an Eldorado of forms and colors that delights the eye and through the eye the mind. Literary imagery speaks from the mind to the eye. It has magic because it is visible without ever seeing the daylight. In the silence of inner life it transmits itself to the senses, and the critic moves about with awe among its vague and remote designs, reflections of earthly realities on a metaphysical plane.

Comparisons between painting and literature have a history of their own. They were of little interest to the Middle Ages in whose well established hierarchy of values painting was set below literature. It was an *ars mechanica*, whereas writing belonged to the liberal arts. [77] Grammar and rhetoric were parts of the *trivium* in the curriculum of scholasticism. During the Renaissance that loosened the solid medieval order and gave great dignity to sensual experience painting came into its own. Dante already had paid tribute to it by calling it a grandchild

---

[76] Leonardo da Vinci, *The Literary Works*, ed. Paul Richter, 2nd ed. (London, New York, Toronto: Oxford University Press, 1939), I, 56.

[77] *Ibid.*

of the Creator. Alberti saw in it a mistress of all the arts, and Leonardo da Vinci considered it superior to poetry. [78]

At the outset of the French sixteenth century the court poet Lemaire de Belges, awakening to the spirit of the times, is spellbound by painting, compares it to literature and interprets it with discernment. [79] He praises the pleasure it affords to the senses. It serves, he says, "pour recreer les yeulx humainz ... / Et pour aux sens volupte concepvoir." [80] Without going as far as Leonardo da Vinci he considers painting an equivalent to literature, certainly a new attitude among the *grands rhétoriqueurs* whose school he perpetuated. In the *Plainte du désiré* a nymph of painting and one of rhetoric appear as fellow-mourners at the body of Duke Louis de Luxembourg-Ligny, one of the patrons of the poet (p. 67). In the *Couronne Margaritique* Lemaire evokes the figure of Martia, a symbol of painting and showers praises upon her. [81] She has her workshop at the court of "King Honor," stands in the service of "Dame Science" and creates masterpieces with a "divine hand" (IV, 154 and 157).

In the *Plainte du désiré* Lemaire practically supports our thesis by his stress on spatial grandeur and variety in painting. Perhaps without knowing it he points thereby at characteristic elements of his own writing and the period altogether. The already mentioned nymph of painting admonishes artists to reproduce nature "Loingtaine à l'œil par bonne perspective" (vs. 218, p. 75). And in the following description of a painter's workshop Lemaire becomes simply dizzy at the sight of the diversity of tools and colors used in the pursuit of the craft:

> Leur ouvroir est tout plein de tableaux
> Peints, et à peindre, et de main noble oustil.
> Là sont charbons, crayons, plumes, pinceaux,
> Brousses à tas, coquilles par monceaux,

---

[78] *Ibid.*

[79] Georges Doutrepont, *Jean Lemaire de Belges et la Renaissance* (Bruxelles, 1934). Jean Frappier, *Jean Lemaire de Belges et les beaux arts* in *Les langues et littératures modernes dans leurs relations avec les beaux arts* (Florence, 1955).

[80] *La plainte du désiré*, ed. D. Yabsley (Paris, 1932), vss. 41-42, p. 77. All parenthetical references pertaining to the above work relate to this edition.

[81] Jean Lemaire de Belges, *Œuvres*, ed. J. Stecher (Louvain, 1882-1891), IV, 56. All parenthetical references pertaining to the *Couronne Margaritique* relate to this edition.

Pinceaux d'argent, qui font maint trait subtil,
Marbres polis, aussi clers que Beryl,
Inde, Azur vert, et Azur de Poulaine,
D'Ancre Azur fin qui du feu n'ha peril,
Et Varmillon, dont mainte boite est pleine.

D'autres couleurs y ha abondamment:
Lacque, Synope, et Pourpre de haut prys:
Fin Or molu, Or Music Orpieument,
Carnation faite bien proprement,
Ocre de Ruth, Machinot, Vert de gris,
Vert de montaigne, et Rose de Paris,
Bon blanc de plomb, Flourec de garance,
Vernis de glace, en deux ou trois barilz,
Et Noir de lampe, estant noir à oultrance.

(p. 158)

Lemaire's affection for painters and their technique is rare even in Renaissance literature. In the *Plainte du désiré* (vss. 113-128, p. 70) and in the *Couronne Margaritique* (IV, 162-163) he mentions by name no less than 22 masters with epithets that reveal his knowledge of their life and work and sometimes a fine understanding of their art. In the former work he stresses the glory of Jean Fouquet (vs. 118), the elegance of Jan van Eyck (vs. 120), the "superior grace" of Leonardo da Vinci (vs. 123), the eternal fame earned by Gentile Bellini (vs. 124); Perugino, says Lemaire, mixes his colors well (vs. 125) and Jean de Paris gives to nature "umbraige et esperitz" (vs. 128). In the *Couronne* he mentions among others Hugo van der Goes "qui eut les tretz netz" (IV, 162), and Marmion who is the "Prince d'enluminure / Dont le nom croist, comme paste de levain / Par les effects de sa noble tournure" (IV, 162).

There is reason to believe that Lemaire was personally acquainted with some of the contemporary painters and that he frequented their workshops. In his youth he may have been in close contact in the city of Valenciennes with Marmion and later in Lyon with Jean Perréal, also known as Jean de Paris.[82] His exceptional interest in painting makes us wonder if at a certain time of his life he did not himself dabble in this art.[83] In a passage of the *Concorde des deux*

---

[82] *La plainte du désiré*, ed. cit., p. 41.

[83] It has been said that he influenced by his writings painting and the tapestries of the Palace of Madrid. *v.* Emile Mâle, *L'Art religieux de la fin du moyen âge en France,* 2nd ed. (Paris, 1922), pp. 342-343.

langages in which he describes himself as having made an illumination in a dream (142-148, p. 35) and the following lines from the *Plainte du désiré* reveal a surprising professional knowledge of colors needed to produce a somber landscape:

> Faictes broyer sur voz poliz porphires
> Couleurs duisans a mon intention,
> Toutes de noir et de diverses tires,
> Pour exprimer les douloureux martires
> Que Nature a par griefve infection.
> Faictes mesler paste carnation:
> Ne desctrempez que noir de flambe ou bistre,
> C'est la couleur qui de deuil est ministre.
> Laissez a part synople et asur d'Acre,
> Lacque, vert gay, toutes haultes couleurs:
> Gardez les bien pour quelque ymaige sacre,
> Pour estoffer statue ou symulachre
> Qui soit de pris et de riches valeurs.
> Icy ne fault que touches de douleurs,
> Car d'or molu Nature ne se pare
> Quant quelque grief de joye la separe.
>
> (vss. 129-144, p. 72) [84]

By his poetic attitude towards artists Lemaire predicts Romanticism, by his feel for color the Parnasse, by the freshness and brightness of his visual impressions on anything connected to painting he probably is unique in French literature.

2. EARLY MANIFESTATIONS OF GROWTH: THE PASTORAL

An analysis of some characteristic French pastorals from the late Middle Ages to the early Renaissance will offer a parallel in literature to the increase of space and variety found in landscape painting, the subject matter of Chapter I. of this study. One work of the fourteenth century, four of the fifteenth and two scenes written by Lemaire de Belges at the beginning of the sixteenth century will illustrate this development. [85]

The spatial aspects of the evolution are beautiful and revealing. The increase in volume follows a straight line of progression leading

---

[84] Frappier, *Jean Lemaire de Belges et les beaux arts*, p. 111.

[85] Alice Hulubei, *L'Eglogue en France au XVIe siècle* (Paris, 1938), pp. 127, 147-150, 153.

from a cozy medieval atmosphere to the first manifestations of a cosmic vision of the world. And while the graphic characteristics of the works differ according to the variety of literary traditions the authors drew from, they blend harmoniously with the principles of spatial representation.

The first of the series, the *Dictz de Franc Gontier,* a short poem by Philippe de Vitry designed to laud the simplicity of country life, has rough and well defined contours and no spatial depth to speak of. The next three fifteenth century works make tentative sallies into the natural background catching an occasional glimpse of the sky and of fairly remote lands. The effect of the distances they evoke is most often counteracted by solid objects in the background that stop the view, so that in their final form the landscapes offer intimacy and peace. Such is the milieu of Christine de Pisan's *Dit de la pastoure* that deals with the amorous adventures of a shepherdess. The limited dimensions of this work fit in with the delicate and limpid lines characteristic of tales of courtly love. [86] The *Banquet du bois,* a fifteenth century elaboration of the story of Franc Gontier, [87] is a little vaguer in its drawing than the original, perhaps because of its greater depth. René d'Anjou's *Regnault et Jehanneton* [88] to be analyzed next, actually is far more voluminous than the previous two, yet remains within the medieval frame. Although it contains conventional elements of rustic life and bucolic love, it is nevertheless highly individualistic and has thanks to its author's affectionate interest in nature great freshness in its drawing. Passages here inserted from Molinet's *Throsne d'honneur* herald in somewhat blurred fashion the spatial grandeur of the Renaissance. This grandeur will appear with great clarity in Lemaire de Belges, who "makes his images visible to the inward eye" as Arthur Tilley observed with a phrase we like to quote. [89] This is manifest in the pastoral scenes of the *Temple d'honneur et de vertus* [90] and of the

---

[86] Marie-Joseph Pinet, *Christine de Pisan* (Paris, 1927), pp. 256-257.

[87] Hulubei, *L'Eglogue en France,* p. 147.

[88] Authorship not conclusively established.

[89] *The Dawn of the French Renaissance* (Cambridge, 1918), p. 345.

[90] Jean Lemaire de Belges, *Temple d'honneur et de vertus,* ed. H. Hornik (Paris, 1957), vss. 1-397, pp. 50-64. This is the passage marked by an eminently pastoral atmosphere. The rest of the poem will be analyzed in the third part of this chapter. All parenthetical references pertaining to the above work relate to this edition.

Illustrations de Gaule et Singularités de Troie [91] that will conclude this part of the study.

With its lack of setting the *Dictz de Franc Gontier* is a striking parallel to fourteenth century paintings:

> Soubs feuille verd, sur herbe délectable
> Sur ruy [92] bruyant et sur clère fontaine
> Trouvay fichée une borde portable [93]
> Là surmangeoient Gontier et Dame Hélaine. [94]

The leaves of the trees above and the grass and river and fountain underneath limit the tableau in both directions, and almost all of the short tale takes place within these confines. At the end of the poem Gontier leaves in order to enter a forest, a medium that stops the view completely.

In the *Dit de la pastoure* the landscape shows a slight increase in depth. It unfolds mildly and sparingly on a horizontal plane and in space. In some of the characteristic scenes meadows that to some extent open the view alternate with forests and groves that reduce it. The following lovely lines introduce the motif in the early part of the poem:

> Trés que jœnne touse estoie,
> Parmi bouscages hantoye
> Et par ces landes sauvages
> Pour repaistre enmi herbages
> Les berbiettes de mon pere. [95]

A few lines below another picture reproduces the same mood:

> D'autre riens n'avoye cure
> Fors de repairier en champs

---

[91] Jean Lemaire de Belges, *Œuvres*, ed. Stecher, *Les Illustrations de Gaule et Singularitez de Troye* (Louvain, 1882-1891), I, 133-202. All parenthetical references pertaining to the *Illustrations* relate to this edition.

[92] *Ruisseau.*

[93] *Cabane portative.*

[94] *Recueil de poésies françoises des XV⁰ et XVI⁰ siècles*, ed. Montaiglon and Rothschild (Paris, 1875), X, 198. All parenthetical references pertaining to the *Dicts de Franc Gontier* relate to the above edition.

[95] Christine de Pisan, *Œuvres poétiques*, ed. Maurice Roy (Paris, 1891), II, vss. 59-63, p. 225. All parenthetical references pertaining to the above work relate to this edition.

Et en bois, ou les doulz chans
Des oysiaulx souvent ouoye.
(vss. 72-75, p. 225)

Scenes of the same kind reappear later in the text (vss. 247-248, p. 231 and vss. 274-275, p. 238). Intimacy is most fully realized at the outset of the amorous adventure. The nobleman who will win the heart of the shepherdess finds her sitting in a forest thick with trees and devoid of sunlight. She is so well hidden that the knight who is attracted by her singing can hardly find her (vss. 453-493, pp. 237-238). This image may be contrasted with a matinal landscape, the most spacious one of the tale. Here the authoress raises her eyes from the earth to the sky:

Au matin que le jour crieve
Pensant a amours me lieve,
A soleil levant m'en vois
O mes berbis vers le bois.
(vss. 1240-1243, p. 261-262)

Interestingly enough the perspective disappears as soon as it has opened. After having seen the protagonist walking under the open sky at sunrise, we lose sight of her as she enters the forest.

A comparison between the *Banquet du bois* and its above discussed fourteenth century model offers an excellent insight into the evolution of spatial representation. A transformation of the subject matter permits the author to move from the interior, the exclusive medium of the original, to the outdoors. The central figure, formerly a woodcutter, turns into a shepherd, and the conventional pastoral plot shows him departing from the four walls of his dwelling where he was confined in the winter out into the open in spring. The story reproduces, as it were, the artistic development of the genre: the sheperd's will to move into nature corresponds to the esthetic aspiration of the author:

Après l'ennuy du mal temps yvernage
Que les buissons prennent nouvelle cotte,
Que les oyseaulx s'esveillent et font rage
De jargonner mainte joyeuse notte,

> Damp Franc Gontier, avecques sa mignotte
> La doulce Hélaine, furent en leur maison. [96]

The meal that was served in the model work inside the cabin now is consumed in the fields. Reminded by his beloved that spring has come, Gontier, after having played his *viele* and his *rebëbe*, invited the rest of the shepherds to a banquet in the open. With all the praises of the beauty of nature that they contain, the descriptions never seem to become vast. The feast takes place "au les d'un bois" (p. 213). The nearness of the forest gives to the scene a note of coziness that is intensified by the fact that a hawthorn covers the gathering place:

> Soubz aubépine bien flourie et flairant
> En lieu amène, comme en ung paradis,
> Manda Gontier, esté tint repairant
> Ly bon bergier et pastour de jadis.
>
> (p. 209)

Reference to the earthly paradise stresses the intimacy of the tableau. Contemporary miniatures reveal that the medieval mind conceived of the Garden of Eden as a small and enclosed area, and therefore a land of supreme happiness and beauty. [97]

That René d'Anjou's *Regnault et Jehanneton* is more spacious than all previously mentioned works is partially due to its theme. [98] The story of a pilgrimage, it necessarily implies some sense of distance and fairly extensive horizontal and vertical dimensions. Yet it too is not very ample. It covers only a two days' journey on foot, and as the wanderer moves along open and sheltered areas interchange in a pleasant rhythmical succession. Thus after having drawn the image of an open plain, the author shows the pilgrim at the edge of a grove (vss. 203-204, p. 46). Such hesitation between distance and visual restraint is found not only in the detail of the description but

---

[96] *Recueil de poésies françoises des XVᵉ et XVIᵉ siècles* (Paris, 1875), X, 206. All parenthetical references pertaining to the *Banquet du bois* relate to this edition.

[97] Kenneth Clark, *Landscape into Art* (London, 1949), p. 4.

[98] Le Roi René, *Regnault et Jehanneton*, ed. Maurice du Bos (Paris, 1923), p. 46. All parenthetical references pertaining to the work relate to this edition.

also in the tableau of the entire first day. René describes spaces in the sunlight and spaces at nightfall with equal pleasure.

During the day representations of flight are essential to the development of volume. At dawn the soaring of the larks makes us raise our eyes and take in the reappearing horizons: "Et d'autre part calandres volleter / Lors commencèrent et en l'air monter" (vss. 36-37, p. 37). During the course of the day slight notations of flight are inserted, which keep us near the surface of the earth, yet add a tridimansional character to the landscape. A kingfisher plunges from a branch into the water to pick up a small fish (vss. 236-259, pp. 49-50). A swallow chases bees in the air (vss. 261-271, p. 50) and a turtle-dove flutters about to meet its mate (vss. 456-499, pp. 62-65).

The effacement of nature in the evening is very moving:

> Le soleil estoit abessant
> Et plus là ne s'estoit moustrant
> Ne nulle part apparaissant,
> Fors qu'au clocher ou quel touchant
> Estoit ung pou resplendissant;
> Mais guères ne le fus voyant
> Car de veue tost le perdis.
>
> (vss. 1060-1066, p. 100)

It was the first time the author raised his eyes towards the sun, but only to make it gradually disappear. Stirred as he is by the dusk he observes the sun even after its disapperance in its weak reflection on the belfry of the church.

Here again birds are used to enrich the visual drama. Just as in the morning we were made to look up to the sky through the soaring of the larks, the descent of the birds at sunset makes us drop our eyes and experience the waning of the universe. Flocks of partridges fall to the ground before darkness sets in:

> Les perdris si se réclamoient
> Et puis en trouppeaulx s'envolloient
> Et à coup ou garet [99] se chéoient
> Et là toute nuit se tenoient.
>
> (vss. 1053-1056, p. 99)

---

[99] guéret, fallow land.

Other birds enter their nests and reproduce in the shelter of their dwellings the general mood of coziness found in the evening:

> Et les gents oiseletz joyeulx
> Plaisans et doulx et amoureulx
> Cessoient leur glay [100] mélodieulx
> Et çà et là chascun qui mieulx
> S'alloient couscher deux à deulx
> Dedans leurs niz très gracieulx,
> Ne plus leurs doulx chans ne chantoient.
>
> (vss. 1039-1045, p. 98)

The author makes the existence of space felt even in the complete darkness of the night. And once more the birds serve to interpret the phenomenon. Screech-owls, we are told, come out of their hollow abodes into the open and bats that have remained hidden from the sun now animate by their flight the invisible cosmos (vss. 1066-1071, p. 100).

The birds are still with us in the description of the following day, a short passage consisting of mere six stanzas. This time swallows fly high up into the air to make us aware of the emergence of the world from darkness:

> Puis le matin, lors que hault clame
> L'aronde à l'aube, ains que nul âme
> Si se levast, fus homme ou fame,
> Ne que luisist du soleil drame,
> ... ...
> Et que le soleil commençat à poindre.
>
> (vss. 1088-1094, p. 102)

Brief as the account of the second day is, it contains nevertheless a total image of the pilgrim's excursion, indeed the only passage that gives us a sweeping view of nature:

> Oultre passay...
> Par mons, par plains et bas et hault
> Cheminay tant, si Dieu me sault
> Que révins dont partir je fus.
>
> (vss. 1119-1121, p. 103)

---

[100] *ramage*, singing, warbling.

The esthetic outlook on nature undergoes a veritable revolution between René d'Anjou and Molinet. The following beautiful passage, the beginning of the *Throsne d'honneur,* presents heaven and earth in one single sentence and could easily have been written in the sixteenth century: "Durant le temps que Titan triumphoit ou signiferant Zodiacque, en haulte spere, approchant le tres glorieux regne du Lyon, pere de douze signes, lorsque tous arbriceaulx sont revestus joyeusement et que les tres doulces lourettes ont plaissantement rendu leurs odeurs, voeullant recreer et esjoïr mes espris et oÿr les melodieux chantz des oisellés, je m'en allay au joly bois, ou je m'endormis assés souefvement soubz ung beau chesne foeullu." [101] This idyllic image on earth within a cosmic landscape is appealing and has very good visibility too. However, as the prose turns into verse the oral effects of the prosody impose themselves at the expense of the scenery:

> Ciel azuré, region aërine,
> Aureïne splendeur reflamboyant,
> Phebus, Phebé et toute estoille fine
> Perisse et fine et soit mise en ruine,
> Grand bruine soit sur terre umbroiant,
> Car le luisant soleil resplendissant,
> Seul nourissant ce bas siecle univers,
> S'est escoué et en terre convers.
>
> (vss. 9-16, p. 38)

We have here a learned game with rhymes and words, a display of brilliance in vocabulary and versification common to all members of the school of the *grands rhétoriqueurs.* [102] The word group *fine, ruine* and *bruine,* and the group *luisant, resplendissant, nourissant,* and finally aërine and *aurëine* are examples of *rimes batelées* or *rimes en écho* or both. Interwoven is a *rime équivoquée* with the repetition of *fine* used in two senses. As they succeed each other quickly and relentlessly, the rhymes pounce on our ears and tend to break up the totality of the visual impression. Yet if we make an effort to extricate the picture from the ambitious forms of versification we will find that the passage presents in a sweeping motion the sky, the aerial

---

[101] Jean Molinet, *Les faictz et dictz,* ed. Noël Dupire (Paris, 1936), I, vss. 1-9, p. 36. Parenthetical references pertaining to the poem relate to this edition.

[102] Raoul Morçay, *La Renaissance* (Paris, 1935), I, 83-84. Henry Guy, *Histoire de la poésie française au XVI*e *siècle* (Paris, 1910), pp. 82-100.

regions underneath it, the sun, the moon, the stars, and a sort of eclipse of the sun that leads up to a startling observation at the end of the lines: the sparkling sun, the poet says, has assumed the color of the earth.

Although Lemaire de Belges adopted in a general way the style of the school his vocabulary is far less imposing in its aural effects and more appropriately chosen as to its meaning. The first verses of the *Temple d'honneur et de vertus* reveal it:

> Donnez repos à vos doulx fajoletz
> Tant mignoletz, gentilz bergiers des champs;
> Et vous aussi, tres plaisans oyseletz,
> Rossignoletz, cessez ung pou vos pletz
> D'amours repletz, pour ouyr autres chantz.
> Ruisseaulx glissans, qui menez brutz plaisans,
> Soyez taisans, courez à doulce noyse,
> Souffrez le loz de haulteur bourbonnoyse.
>
> (vss. 3-8, p. 50)

The influence of Molinet and his fellow-poets is obvious. The words *fajoletz* and *mignoletz* form a *rime batelée* and they are echoed in a whole series of adjectives and verbs with a similar ending in lines 3 and 5: with *oyseletz, rossignoletz, cessez, pletz* and *repletz*. In the following two lines three present participles rhyme with one another: *glissans, plaisans,* and *taisans.* With regard to their vocal aspects, however, the words are less turbulent than they were in Molinet. They are inobtrusive and gentle, and far from interfering with the drawing, they partake in their character and thereby enrich it.

With Lemaire's limpid presentation of spatial grandeur we now are actually in the Renaissance. The volume spreads in a horizontal and vertical sense and it is promoted by symbolic objects common to the *rhétoriqueurs.* The horizontal dimensions of the tableau develope from pure personifications, from the figures of seven shepherds and shepherdesses, everyone of whom represents a section of the huge holdings of the Duke of Bourbon and his wife Anne de France, in whose service they are supposed to stand and whose praises they sing. A large geographical section of France around the *Massif Central* thereby unfolds before our eyes. It comprises Beaujolais, Marche, Clermont-en-Beauvoisis, Auvergne, Bourbonnais, Gien and Le Forez.

The scene rises above the earth, particularly in the description of the winds, of Boreas the north wind, Vulturnus the south-west wind,

Circuis the north-west wind and Nothus the south wind. Actually three-dimensional rather than vertical phenomena they take us into various directions of the compass. The symbolic elements of the description lead into the astral regions of the world. The duchess, Anne de Beaujeu, symbolized by Aurora, the dawn, evokes the sky. In a lovely passage she is described as reigning over the planets in golden splendor, spreading light through the clouds and the fog (vss. 295-298, p. 61). At another point Aurora cried because she cannot see Titan the sun, here a symbol of her brother King Charles VIII. The poet consoles her with the following words:

> Or plus n'en plourez
> Belle aux crins dorez;
> Se le desirez
> Veoir, vous le verrez
> Dessus les neuf cieulx.
> Les cieulx azurez,
> Painctz et coulourez,
> Où vous vous mirez
> En sont honnourez
> Au plaisir des dieux.
>   (vss. 253-262, p. 59) [103]

Three aspects of the sky which are superimposed on one another, as it were, mingle in these interesting lines: the visible sky, the astronomically conceived sky, and the image of heaven. The poet's imagination goes back and forth between these media. At the outset we can see the dawn, then the nine spheres that direct the motion of the stars through space. Then above the spheres appears the abode of the blessed souls that brings us back through association to the

---

[103] It is possible for the dawn not to see the sun according to the concepts of Greek mythology. Eos and Titan are distinct realities to the eye: the former vanishes when the latter appears on the sky. In a passage of the *Illustrations* to be discussed Lemaire describes Eos walking ahead of Titan dispersing darkness. But he disregards in our passage mythology by calling Titan the brother of Eos. He may have been influenced by various kinds of other relations between Eos and individuals whose names are similar or identical with Titan. Tytan Hyperion was the father of Eos, Titan Astraeus was her lover and so was Tithonus, the latter being often identified with Titan the sun god. Lemaire also makes casual use of contemporary astronomical theory that places the sun within the fourth of the ten spheres and not above them. Of course Titan had to reach above the material universe in order to meet the duchess when she will be in heaven.

tangible world. The blue of the sky is easily evoked by the idea of heaven which falls down like a curtain in front of the scientific and religious universe. The last phase of the composition shows the dawn looking into the blue sky as if into a mirror.

Representations of Pan, the symbol of the duke, are rarer and have less sensuous impact. They are suggestive, mysterious, all-encompassing. Pan's exterior reflects the entire cosmos. The pipe he plays is attuned to the seven planets (vs. 140, p. 55). He is the embodiment of nature and his clothing is the starry sky: "Pan a manteau de couleur purpurine, / Fort riche et digne ainsi que ung corps celeste, / Tout parsemé de mainte estoille fine..." (vss. 151-153, p. 55).

The pastoral scenes of the *Illustrations de Gaule et Singularités de Troie* show even a greater increase in the size of spacial representations. These chapters partake in the character of the work as a whole, a poeto-historical account highly influenced by Giovanni Nanni, called Annius of Viterbo. [104] Since it was the author's intention to show that the people of Gaule go back to the early periods of mankind, [105] a vague image of the Mediterranean, its islands and surrounding lands emerge from the first twenty chapters of the work as a site of this evolution. At this point the dispassionate chronicle turns into a tale. Within the mute geographic tableau appears a picturesque image of Troy. The author maintains, however, his broad visual perspective. He keeps looking at the subject matter from above, as if suspended in space. In the fifteenth century pastorals and the previously discussed work of Lemaire the authors remained on the ground, their vision being limited by the surrounding milieu. Now we see a great expanse of land near the Hellespont — today's Dardanelles — with the mountain range Ida nearby, from which two rivers, the Xanthus and the Simois flow into the plain of Troy "laquelle ha grand et plantureux espace entre la mer, et les monts" (I, 137). Distances between various elements of the panorama impress themselves upon the reader. The great city of Troy stands at 1500 "steps" from the sea (I, 137). Four or five leagues away from Troy is Sebrene whose pastures reach up to the mountains. Nymphs are dwelling in the riverbed and fountains of the mountains. They descend the slopes in

---

[104] Doutrepont, *Jean Lemaire de Belges et la Renaissance* (Bruxelles, 1934), p. 15.
[105] *Ibid.*, p. 271.

order to admire the beauty of youthful Paris who lives among the shepherds in the plain (I, 142). No previous French pastoral is quite as large and airy — the traditional coziness of the genre is gone.

In some of the successive passages aerial and cosmic images make their appearance. While describing the month of August the author's eyes wander from the sky down to earth and then upward again into the air. The description starts out with an astronomical observation of the sun and the constellations in the Zodiac, then it becomes earthbound. Passing in front of Virgo, Titan, the sun, looks down at the harvestin goddess, Ceres, while the countryside and the air resound with the singing of cicadas and crickets that hide in the stubblefields or bushes. A graceful east wind, the Eurus, seems to alleviate the heat which covers the landscape with a haze (I, 184). At another point the author offers an epic description of a sunset at sea: "Le beau Phebus commançant à baisser son chariot devers Occident, pour plonger ses cheveux ardans es undes de Tethys..." (I, 190). Particularly fine is a melancholy autumnal landscape in which winds are described passing over forests and frozen rivers: "Et quand ce vint que le riche temps dautomne eut mis en grenier tout son tresor... et que tous arbres furent despouillez de leur beauté verdissante, Vulturnus le froid vent venant de septentrion, comme precurseur, vint annoncer triste nouvelle de froidure hyvernalle, et sifflant de sa grieve alaine, escroloit les gros troncz des hautes forestz" (I, 193). The winds give volume to the scene, and the forests give body to the volume.

In literature as in painting increase of space goes hand in hand with increase in variety. There are of course differences between the two media of expression. The repetition of identical objects frequently found in fifteenth century paintings cannot possibly materialize in writing. Therefore, multitudinousness and variety that to some extent could be discussed separately in painting form a single theme in literature. However, the main aspects of evolution remain the same. In the medieval mood the process of multiplication is slow and comfortable. It is marked by the author's desire to stay within limits. The Renaissance adds detail to detail in its impetuous drive towards the endless.

Characteristic of the pastoral are the enumerations of edibles served at outdoor feasts, most of which are plain and unprepared agricultural products, such as milk, butter, cheese, onions, aromatic herbs, fruits and eggs. These meals, supposed to illustrate the simplicity of country life in contrast with life in lordly residences, [106] appear nevertheless abundant, thanks to the enumerative style used in describing them. They show that to those who live near nature the fertility of the land suffices to provide a copious and delicious repast. In the *Dict de Franc Gontier,* the first one in our list, *Dame Hélaine* serves her woodsman:

> Fromage frais, laict, beure, fromagée,
> Cresme, maton, [107] prune, noix, pomme, poire,
> Cibor, [108] oignon, escalogne froyée [109]
> Sur crouste grise, au gros sel, pour mieulx boire.
>
> (p. 198)

As expressed in the words, "fromage frais" stress is laid in such passages on freshness to which the concept of tidiness is sometimes added; both qualities are evidently absent at the table of the rich. In the *Banquet du bois* whose very title shows the importance of the food motif, a neat and sweetly smelling table cloth is brought along by Helen to be laid out on the grass. The enumeration here is slowed down by adjestives and modifying phrases which are explicatory and endearing, and refer to the abundance and the quality of the meal while stressing at the same time its unpretentiousness. The subject matter has crystallized, the style has become more eloquent:

> Pour honnorer plus haultement le jour,
> Chargea Gontier Hélaine expressément
> Qu'elle aportast, sans y faire séjour,
> Laict et frommaige et sel gros largement,
> La blanche nappe, sentant souefvement,
> Et le beau pain, qui deux fois fust sassé;
> D'autre plus bis se fust-on bien passé.
>
> Aulx et oignons y eut à grosses bottes,
> Et molz frommages en grande quantité,
> Herbes, cyvoz, poirette et eschalottes...
>
> (p. 214)

---

[106] Pierre d'Ailly, "Combien est misérable la vie du Tyran" *Recueil de poésies françoises* (Paris, 1875), pp. 202-203.

[107] Lait aigre et caillé.

[108] Ciboule.

[109] Echalote broyée.

In *Regnault et Jehanneton* whose author was a gourmet, there is a longer list of foodstuffs and more tableware, which is made of primitive material to be sure, so that it should fit the rustic occasion. Ham and mushrooms are added to the tidbits, and two wooden saucetureens, two earthen goblets, and a bowl made of the bark of oak trees help to improve the style of the banquet (vss. 404-427, pp. 59-60).

Christine de Pisan expresses a similar taste for variety, but applies it to other domains, often in a descriptive rather than enumerative tone. At one point she discusses in detail the contemporary military outfit and armor. And the following lines that deal with the tending of sheep recall in their placidity the agricultural scenes of the *Très riches heures du Duc de Berry* by the Limbourg Brothers, particularly the "Month of July" that has a similar theme:

> Si savoye tous les tours
> Du mestier de bergerie:
> Aigniaulx en la bergerie
> Soignier, mettre fein en creche,
> Semer en toit paille fresche
> Et les mottons d'une part
> Trier, oindre et mettre a part
> Berbis traire, et faire a heure
> Aigneulx teter, et desseure
> Le fourrage es rastiaulx mestre;
> ... ...
> Savoye, et mes berbis tondre
> En may assise en belle onbre.
>   (vss. 78-96, p. 226)

In the descriptions of nature of *Regnault et Jenanneton* variety reaches its climax among fifteenth century pastorals. Captivated by the copiousness of animal life the author makes loving observations on a notable number of birds, insects, fish and sometimes fourlegged animals too. Although visibly delighted by the opulence of the scene, he imparts his impressions with a calm and temperance that do not even remotely resemble the Renaissance.

In some of the passages the landscape evolves with an interesting rhythm of its own. Enumerations are often preceded and followed by a more leisurely examination of the phenomena. It appears that while absorbed in the beauty of a certain spectacle the poet quite suddenly is overwhelmed by its multitudinousness. Characteristic in this respect is a series of eight stanzas in the early part of the poem (vss. 36-91, pp. 37-40). In the first three the poet discusses the lark, its fight, its song, its gayety, its feel for harmony. The following stanza belongs to the thrush and the finch. The next one is enumerative and simply abounds with flies of all sorts, crickets, cicadas, butterflies, mosquitoes and scarabaeuses. Then the mood becomes peacefully contemplative again. Attention is focused on a little frog seen in a shallow water near the shore whose voice is comparable to that of a lute. The last two stanzas of the group deal with wild pigeons who like to stay out of men's sight and whose voice is plaintive and smooth. In another part of the work (vss. 213-238, pp. 45-50) the author enjoys the sight of a gently flowing water surrounded by grass and violets. Then he is struck by a large number of fish he can see in the water: loaches, minnows, eels, trouts, roaches and salmon. And once again he is amused and calmed by the manoeuvres of a kingfisher in pursuit of small fish.

In a beautiful scene we have analyzed from the point of view of space René observes life at nightfall. In a mood that is neither too slow nor too speedy he mentions a number of birds and animals, each of which is followed by a short notation on their behaviour: the quail raises its voice in the meadows and the nearby forests resound its tune. The stag leaves the forest and feeds in the wheatfield. Partridges fly around in flocks, drop to the ground and stay in the same spot all night. The stag-beetle flies around noisily, the rabbits trot and leap at the same time, says René (vss. 1046-1059, pp. 98-99).

Here, as in the evolution of space, we are with Molinet at the threshold of the Renaissance. And perhaps more so. While the sound effects of his versification interfere, as observed, with the total view of his scenes, they actually underline the visual amplitude of his individual descriptions that goes far beyond anything the fifteenth century pastoral produced. The reverberation caused by the quick and frequent repetition of the same rhyme creates a strong impression of multitudinousness, but also of variety through the contrast between the identity of the ultima and differences between the preceding syllables. In the following verse taken from the *Throsne d'honneur* the author enumerates a long list of nations interspersed with private names and with words chosen above all for the purpose of increasing the sound effects. The multitude of objects thus assembled are supported by the *rimes batelées* and by echoing rhymes that rumble through the stanza, the first set ending in "-ons" or "ions", the second in "ois"; somewhat hidden in the second and third verse is the pair "Flamens" and "Roland" that also rhymes:

> O Bourguignons, plourés par millions,
> Hardis lions, Flamens, Luxembourgeois,
> Picars, Rolans, Hayniers, Scipïons,
> Fors champions, plourés grans sapions;
> Rocz et pions, Brebanchons, Namurois,
> Tordez vos dois, Hollandois, Zellandois,
> Et Frisonnois, arrestés vos escluses:
> Mouilliés les yeux de vos faces confuses.

> (vss. 105-112, p. 41)

From the point of view of variety the section of Lemaire's *Temple d'honneur* here under discussion is not characteristic of the Renaissance, but reverts to earlier fifteenth century pastorals, with the exception of one passage whose imagery and versification reminds of Molinet (vss. 85-94, p. 53). [110] In the pastoral scenes of the *Illustrations,* however, pleasure taken in variety is highly indicative of the new period. Listings of all sorts, of animals, birds, fruit trees and agricultural implements emerge from the text. (I, 135, 151, 154, 160, 201, 202).

One of the passages is of particular interest, since it borders on the High Renaissance. Lemaire describes with delight and admiration Paris' proficiency in all sorts of physical activties and in music, both of which serve as clear manifestations of the often discussed many-sided individual in the Burckhardtien sense. While generally ascribed to individualism, this phenomenon also must be considered as an expression of the general drive toward diversification. With his exuberance and wonder at human excellence Lemaire here predicts Gargantua's education (I, 23), although no mention is made of studies, a domain in which Paris' masters, the shepherds, evidently were not ready to offer any training: "Nature ... luy administroit agilité et force correspondante à sa beauté ... tout ce qu'il veoit faire aux autres il lapprenoit de leger, voire et en brief les surmonta, aumoins

---

[110] The *Couronne Margaritique* on the contrary offers variety with hardly any spatial effects. The work is of minor interest to our subject and will not be discussed in any detail.

ceux de son aage, fust à ietter la pierre à la main, et à la la fronde,
à tirer la boule, à luitter, à courir, à saillir, ou à noer, aussi à son-
ner cors, chalemeaux, harpes, reberbes, et musettes pastorales. Et
souverainement à tirer de larc, au plus loing et au plus droit, à
chevaucher et dompter chevaux. Et aussi il fut quelque peu instruit en
lecture et en escriture" (I, 134). The introductory sentence of the
quote contains a further Renaissance ideal that also should be associated with variety: the aspiration to identify physical worth with
beauty. Music by its very nature comprises both. Athletics require
them in Greek and Renaissance ways of thinking.

Multifariousness in the human individual is related in the author's
mind to the abundance found in nature. While describing in eloquent
tones the thick forests, the mountains and wastelands, fast moving
rivers and little wells and fountains, snake-filled fields and the grass
and the flowers and the rich animal life of the region, the author,
intoxicated by the spectacle he has created, compares it with the horn
of king Alcinous and the garden of the Hesperides "qui est comme
un Paradis terrestre en Afrique" (I, 174). It was almost to be expected that the author would bring in the cornucopia, a current symbol
and an eloquent expression of diversity due to fertility.

Pegasis Oenone herself reflects copiousness in nature in her very
exterior and attire (I, 66). Lemaire here reproduces an aspect of
thought that is difficult for the Christian mind to comprehend: the
identification of natural phenomena with their divinities. He uses
the image only occasionally and merely approaches it when speaking
of nymphs who "preside" over a fountain or "own" it. The goddesses thus conceived are individuals, and do not unite with matter.
But Pegasis Oenone's father "is" a river (I, 175), and she herself
"is" nature (I, 166). Her head is covered with laurel, her magic dress
with birds and flowers. Harmoniously sounding little bells at the
fringes of her dress reproduce the sound of her fountain. In her hand
she holds a basket made of hosier and her pumps are woven with the
rush of marshes. The color and expression of her eyes retains the blue
of the sky and the flowery green of the shores: "Et le regard d'iceluy
estoit de variable plaisance, semblable à la superficialité dun ruis-
selet, entrechangeant la gaye verdeur et florissance de ces rives avec-
que lazuree beauté du ciel, laquelle y est ioyeusement reverberee"
(I, 166).

The nymphs here described associate in a general way with fertility and variety in nature. The Dryades personify the forests, the Oreades the mountains and hills, the Naiades the rivers, the Hamadriades the trees and shrubs, the Hymnides the grass and flowers, and the Napaeae — Pegasis Oenone is one of them — the fountains (I, 172-174). The plant life described in connection with the nymphs adds to the general impression of plenitude. The Dryads are dwelling "parmy les bois fueilluz et les forestz espesses" (I, 178). The Hymnides "Font verdoyer lherbe haute et drue parmy les prairies, et espanir les diverses flourettes au long les rivages" (I, 172). The pictorial variety is reflected in the aural effects of the vocabulary, in the name of those nymphs that end in the suffix "'ade." The repetition of the suffix together with differences in the base of the words link up with the general drive toward multitudinousness and diversity.

3. NATURE IN MOURNING AND NATURE IN A DREAMLAND

Lemaire's descriptions of death and dreams bear upon each other as expressions of despair and of hope, and they form a harmonious whole. The themes turn up in the second and third section of the *Temple d'honneur et de vertus*. [111] After the first part which was discussed in the previous chapter and which depicts the life of Lemaire's patron Peter II. Duke of Bourbon, the author shows nature in a turmoil at his death. The third part describes within a dream of the duke's widow, a ceremony destined to give him an exalted position among his ancestors and in history. These passages are done with exquisite artistry. The stormy landscape has sharp and clean outlines, the dreamy one is elusive and delicate in its drawing. The scope of our findings will be enlarged by another dream, the subject matter of Lemaire's *Concorde des deux langages*.

Both subjects have long lasting traditions. The concept of nature in a state of disturbance at the death of an eminent personality goes back to the *New Testament* [112] and has in Roman antiquity a

---

[111] Madame Hulubei in *L'Eglogue en France au XVIe siècle* (pp. 156-162) and Hornik in his edition of the *Temple d'honneur et de vertus* (p. 17) agree that the work consists ot two parts. They consider the section that deals with the duke's life and his death a unit, and the dream another. It is our contention that from the point of view of mood and presentation the opus must be divided into three and that the second and third part have more in common than the first and second.

[112] Matthew, XXVIII, 51-52.

splendid literary expression in Ovid's description of Caesar's death. [113] In France we have it in its early form in the *Chanson de Roland*. [114] In the fifteenth century it may have received new impetus as a special version of the then prevalent interest in the portrayal of the physical aspects of death as found in the poetry of Villon and in woodcuts representing the *Danse Macabre*. [115] The theme here moves from the image of the decaying human body to a gruesome vision of the exterior world, of nature seen in a sudden state of decomposition. The genre has been cultivated extensively by the *grands rhetoriqueurs*. [116] As far as the symbolic dreams are concerned they are related as regards style and presentation to medieval works of the type of the *Roman de la rose*. The allegorical temples described in the dreams have an even richer past. Marked by a variety of literary styles they appear in a large number of writings in classical and Christian literature. In France Guillaume de Lorris, Froissart, Chastellain, Molinet and many others made it their own. [117] Both genres differ in Lemaire de Belges from their medieval predecessors by their large spatial effects and by their variety.

Lemaire's description of nature in a state of turbulence involves heaven and earth, and extends considerably in both a vertical and horizontal sense. As contrary to his other landscapes that are essentially bright, the author here creates impressions of distance in a darkened universe, an awesome experience of the eye.

---

[113] *Metamorphoses*, XV, 779-801.

[114] Chap. 110.

[115] Huizinga, *The Waning of the Middle Ages* (London, 1924), pp. 124-135.

[116] Floyd Gray, "Variations on a Renaissance Theme: The Poetic Landscape and a *Stance* of Agrippa D'Aubigné, *Philological Quarterly*, XLIV (1965), 437. The lament as a genre has been cultivated by most *rhétoriqueurs*, by Robertet, Octavien de Saint Gelais, Simon Greban, Guillaume Crétin, André de la Vigne, Jean Marot, Molinet, etc. Lemaire himself who had the misfortune of loosing several of his patrons wrote no less than five. His *Regretz de la dame infortunee* written to express the grief of Marguerite d'Autriche at the loss of her brother Philippe-le-Beau contains a darkened landscape similar to the one here discussed, but much shorter. It will not be analyzed here since it does not add new aspects to our study. *v.* for more information Lemaire de Belges, *La plainte du désiré*, ed. D. Yabsley (Paris, 1932), pp. 31-32 and Henry Guy, *Histoire de la poésie française au seizième siècle* (Paris, 1910), I, Chapters 205, 284-292, 382, 392-396, 406-429, 490, 500, 533, 590-591.

[117] *Le temple d'honneur et de vertus*, ed. cit., pp. 35-39.

Let us observe that Lemaire draws on Molinet's already mentioned "Throsne d'honneur" which unfolds the image of a cosmos of great size. He divides it like the Platonists into three: a celestial, an astral and a terrestrial region. At first God and the angels can be seen in heaven. Next comes the description of a sky darkened through the extinction of all sources of light, an eclipse of the sun, the moon and the stars. Within the great obscurity that ensues the author gives us a feel of the presence of space through motion, a steady rainfall and the blowing of winds: Aeolus, Zephyrus and Boreas are called upon to move about in every direction. [118]

Lemaire, who, as mentioned before, achieves greater visual clarity than his master, Molinet, gives in the *Temple d'honneur et de vertus* to the supernatural element somewhat les prominence, but uses it to good advantage. At a certain point the tableau turns into the image of an unusually stormy but altogether possible autumn day, the season in which the duke actually died. The description starts with the motion of stars in an astrological medium. No eclipse takes place but the constellations predict evil. The conjunction of Mars and Saturn obstructed the light of Jupiter and augured ill (vss. 398-415, pp. 64-65). Furthermore the sun left the constellation of Libra and entered that of Scorpio, an event that filled the air with poison and gall, says the author, although at this point he refers to the usual motion of heavenly bodies in the fall (vss. 509-510, p. 68 and vss. 519-525, p. 69).

The rest of the passage can be divided into three parts, the first of which precedes the duke's death, the second coincides with it, and the third follows it.

The first is the most spacious and agitated of the three (vss. 392-519, pp. 64-69). It goes from the astral milieu through the air to the surface of the earth and there spreads out horizontally. All parts of the universe here depicted are marked by melancholia, wrath, physical deformities, and obscurity. The seven spheres are horrible and angered (vs. 422, p. 65): the sky is "swelled" and underneath it the air is "repulsive, troubled, black and bloated" (vs. 419, p. 65). In the general obscurity sudden light effects and the sound and motion of the winds that whistle with "draconic furor" through the world

---

[118] Jean Molinet, *Les faictz et les dictz* (Paris, 1936), I, 36-56.

make space seem perceptible. Very good is a description of flashes
of light in the darkness as manifestations of latent anger:

> Nous avons veu en l'air flambes patentes,
> Estoilles chœir, planettes scintiller
> En demonstrant les grands yres latentes.
>
> (vss. 446-448, p. 66)

Animals' exterior, movements and voices add to the general dismay
and thus serve to bring the imagery down to the surface of the earth
as well as to the space immediately above it and under the ground.
Here, too, the author creates impressions of spatial expansion in darkness. He intimates rather than points clearly at the presence of creatures dispersed all over the region. Some he identifies by their sound
rather than by visual realities: dogs were howling, bulls were roaring
pitifully, revens were croaking and roosters were crowing at unusual
hours. At one point a substantial and rather clearly drawn image is
dimmed down at the end of the description to fit the general atmospheric conditions. The wolves we are told kill the sheep and
strangle mastiffs; and if the commotion continues, they may also attack
people like "wild and hungry goblins" (vs. 649, p. 73). By comparing
the wolves to specters the author produces an impression of obscurity.
As in the spaces above, motion serves to interpret the dark aerial
expanse near the earth. The flight of screech-owls is appropriately
chosen for that purpose: "nous avons veu les chatz huans voler /
Autour des parcz" (vss. 449-450, p. 66). Creatures arising from the
ground or from below it give spatial depth to the description. Snakes
hidden in the grass bite the shepherds unexpectedly (vss. 456-460,
p. 66). And everywhere hideous monsters appear from underneath the
earth spreading terror among men (vss. 470-472, p. 67).

The second section that shows nature at the moment of the duke's
death contrasts with the first by its expressive silence and calm (vss.
520-606, p. 69-71). After its horrible omens the catastrophe itself sets
in quietly. Darkness now is the outstanding characteristic of the landscape. It is produced by a black cloud, a harbinger of death, that is
brought by the north wind, and stopped on top of the hut of Pan, the
symbol of the duke throughout the work. The passage is dramatic:

Tout lentement, sans fouldre et sans tonnoire,
Venoit la triste, obscure, tenebreuse
La nyeble brune, horrible exterminoire.

(vss. 535-537, p. 69)

While describing how it discolors the exterior of animals and men,
Lemaire gives a general impression of the space covered by darkness:

La noire nue avoit de tous costez
Çaint le pourpris et tainct de sa couleur
Brebis, aigneaulx, pasteurs desconfortez.
Tous les troupeaulx en signe de douleur,
En obscur noir changerent toisons blanches
Et les bergiers prindrent dueil et pasleur.

(vss. 556-561, p. 70)

The third passage completes the composition on a harmonious
note. After an agitated introduction and a motionless middle part that
marks the fact of death, the tale is cathartically concluded with the
description of a prolonged autumnal rainfall. Although clouded and
dreary the mood of the landscape here is altogether more restful. The
volume remains large, depicting the sky, the mountains, and the earth.
Returning to a symbol used earlier in the work and raising his eyes
to the heights, Lemaire identifies the duchess with the dawn and
interprets the steady rain as an endless flow of her tears (vss. 575-
585, pp. 70-71). High up in the mountains the rain turns into snow
while in the valleys the rivers swell up "par grant desdaing" (vs. 608,
p. 72), overflowing the meadows and changing the "beautiful carpet
of flowers into mud" (vs. 618, p. 72). The scene ends with the description of nightfall that envelops the already saddened world:

Puis, tost apres, la nuyt feit couverture
A l'air obscur de ses grands esles brunes
Et feit au jour unbrageuse closture.

(vss. 625-627, p. 72)

The metaphor likening darkness to a winged creature has force and
beauty. By giving body to a mere optical phenomenon the author
covers and fills the invisible world with a pseudo matter thereby stressing the presence of space and appealing to our senses. A similar poetic
scheme can be found in descriptions of Remy Belleau.

In the dream of the duchess that follows the death scene (vss. 641-1417, pp. 73-100) large spatial effects materialize in the author's presentation of a mountain and in his description of flight. The mountain, a lovely faint structure that belongs to the world of dreams, is narrow and extremely tall. It reaches above the clouds, as it should, since it serves as a base for the celebrations held in praise of the duke's virtue whose reputation "pierces the sky" (vs. 655, p. 73): "Comme il luy sembla, furent en ung moment transportez sur une montaigne haulte et spectable dont le sommet surpassoit de beaucoup les nues errans et la region aerine. Si estoit icelluy mont semblable a celluy qu'on nomme Olympus en Macedone" (668-673, p. 74). In the temple that stands on top of the mountain the duke will take his place in his ancestry and in eternal life. Since we actually are in the abode of the blessed souls, the author faces a dilemma in his efforts to make the traditional image of the mountain fit his tale. To place the heavenly paradise on top of a mountain is an absurdity. He, therefore, mingles Greek mythology with Christianity and his temple becomes a synthesis of Olympus and heaven.

From the description of this frail mountain the author proceeds to the representation of flight to give us a feel of spatial depth. A symbolic figure called *Entendement* and identified as a *paranymphe* appears in the dream. After having addressed the duchess he takes to the air in order to inform prominent individuals of the "glorious enthronement and the celestial exaltation" (1294-1295, p. 96) of her husband. In an effort to give to this abstraction visual clarity, Lemaire once more mingles classical antiquity with Christianity. The figure resembles an angel, but he also has wings on his arms and heels, and thereby recalls Mercury, a messenger himself (807-811, p. 79). A comparison of his flight with that of birds helps to visualize him in space. To characterize his speed the author likens him at one point to an eagle (1223, p. 93), at another to a swallow (1301-1302, p. 96). The territory he covers is large, for he visits Louis XII, King of France, Philibert Duke of Savoie, Philip Archduke of Austria, Charles Duke of Gelderland and Jeanne de France, Duchess of Berry. At the end of the passage flight through space is replaced by the motion of sound through space. The winged messenger stops on a mountain near Lyon where he makes his announcement to the whole neighborhood, raising his "firm and resounding voice" so that he can be heard several leagues away (1346-1347, p. 98).

In the dream contained in the *Concorde des deux langages* Lemaire uses similar graphic means in order to develop an altogether different theme. He reproduces his personal experiences through the use of symbols. Ejected from the temple of Venus he seeks and finds consolation in the temple of Minerva. The tableau is larger and richer and yields three main motifs. In addition to the mountain motif he offers a landscape which is depicted by the motion of objects through space. In a succession of charming passages the author is finally able to build up visual impressions through sound effects.

The two mountains that serve as a setting for the temples differ in size. The temple of Venus is placed on an existing hill, evidently the hill Fourvière near Lyon at the confluence of the Rhône and Saone, and has natural proportions. [119] With the temple of Minerva we are back in the sky and the clouds:

> Vecy le noble roch qui les nuës surpasse,
> De plus haulx montz qu'on saiche au monde l'outrepasse,
> Dont le sommet attaint l'air du ciel tressalubre.
>
> (vss. 1-3, p. 39)

The landscape referred to contains images of heavenly bodies, of mythological figures, of birds and winds. It reaches from the sky down to the earth. The sun is seen entering the Ram through the arches of the Zodiac (vss. 64-65, p. 10). Further down the goddess Venus appears in the air surrounded by gods of laughter in a chariot driven by doves and swans (vss. 43-51, p. 9). A conventional image of Roman antiquity, it is fresh and alive just the same, couched as it is in a description of the incipient spring. As so often in Lemaire's works the winds make the air tangible. The north wind Boreas stops its blasts, and Auster, the south wind, no more raises from the abyss of the sea its dark storm clouds. Both give way to gentle Zephyrus (vss. 58-63, p. 9). In the end Flora covers the warm earth with roses and columbines. Thus in its final effect the scenery spreads out in the two-dimensional plane.

The evocation of distance which is realized through the travel of sound is the keynote of passages attached to the apparition of Venus.

---

[119] Jean Lemaire de Belges, *La concorde des deux langages*, ed. Jean Frappier (Paris, 1947), XXX-XXI. All parenthetical references pertaining to this work relate to this edition.

They deal with the song of birds, with musical instruments played on earth and on Olympus, and with the music of the spheres. Tonal reverberation is one of the phenomena here described. The sound of flageolets and bagpipes played by the shepherds resound on the high mountains (vss. 82-84, p. 10). Similarly the walls of the temple of Venus resound from above the sweet canticle of the birds whose tune is broken up by chords (vss. 221-222, p. 16). Sometimes music rises towards distant objectives, pointing at them rather than reaching them. Thus "the throats of little birds" greet Aurora as she appears in the sky (vs. 125, p. 12). At another point a joyful and tremendous concert given by a variety of birds mounts heavenward: "Leurs poinctz d'orgues volerent aux haulx cieulx" (vs. 232, p. 17). His vision lifted by sound, as it were, the poet now moves from the surface of the earth up to Olympus, where the gods are seen and heard playing musical instruments and singing in association with birds that carol below. In a zig-zag motion the scene moves down to earth and then far up into space again. Observations on the superiority of modern music over times past bring the poet back to earth. He praises some contemporary French and Flemish composers. In a state of ecstasy he summons the music of the spheres, so that the description ends in the cosmos:

> Les neuf beaux cieulx que Dieu tourne et tempere
> Rendent tel bruit en leurs spheres diffuses
> Que le son vient jusqu'en nostre hemispere.
>
> (vss. 262-264, p. 18) [120]

Because of the multitude of sources used in gathering material these passages are characteristic of the Renaissance interest in variety. The poet transforms his rich and diverse sources [121] into a harmonious though expressly variegated whole.

At the enthronement of the duke in the temple of honor and virtue (983-1220, pp. 85-93) military heroes, orators, historians, and poets appear in person. Some come from the Bible, others from Greek and Roman mythology, and again others from historical Italy and France. They are forty-seven in number and meet face to face with the duke

---

[120] v. on Lemaire and music: Lemaire de Belges, *La plainte du désiré*, pp. 37-39.

[121] Jean Frappier, "Jean Lemaire de Belges et les beaux arts," *Les langues et littératures modernes dans leurs relations avec les beaux arts* (Florence, 1955), p. 112.

and duchess' ancestry, kings and queens, princes and princesses, counts, bishops, archbishops, and primates, twenty-five of whom are identified by name. David stands next to Hector, Simon Greban, Scipio, Constantine, King René, Livi, Charlemagne, Boccaccio, Seneca, and Meschinot. Twelve more persons of all sorts and origins appear by way of conversation. And at the death of the duchess, the author adds not without relish that even more people will be present. Some members of the dynasty, mostly from the family of Bourgogne and Bourbon, have escorted the duke into the temple; the rest of them are arranged in a hierarchical pyramid inside the building. And when Saint Louis, founder of the family of the *Bourbonnais*, puts a crown of glory on the newcomer's head, all those present stand up for the ceremony in a *doulx tumulte* (1102, p. 89), an understatement due to the author's respect for the supposedly gentle manners of high nobility and of the great names in history.

A poetic passage of the *Concorde*, which we have analyzed from the point of view of space is remarkable also for its variety. It combines in a prodigious synthesis images of singing birds with mythological individuals who sing and play musical instruments and with fifteenth century composers (vss. 220-270, pp. 16-18). The theme has medieval antecedents but is new in its presentation. In this wonderful hodge-podge, nightingales, swallows, blackbirds, mavis, canaries, siskins, goldfinch, linnets and jays are found in the company of the Greek poets Terpander and Arion, of Pythagoras considered a musician, of the mythological musicians Orpheus, Amphion, Linos, Thamyras and Thubal, and of the composers Alexander Agricola, Josquin, Ockeghem, and Loÿset Compère. Scores of musical realities with visual impact add to the diversity of the tableau. Descriptions of singing birds appeal to the eye of the reader. Some sing the countertenor, others execute a cadence or chant a canticle. Some modulate their voices, some use diminution to ornament their tune. Many form choral groups intoning some medieval genre, chirping along in alternate verses, harmonizing different rhythmical systems or presenting a musical dispute, the so-called *tenzon*. A number of musical instruments are also mentioned: the viol, the vielle, the harp, the flageolet, the guiterna, the psaltery, the decacorde, and the manicorde.

Another passage of the *Concorde* previously discussed builds up to multitudinousness by a combination of mythological gods and symbolic images (vss. 40-132, pp. 9-12). Within a rather charming description of nature Venus, Phoebus, Flora, the god Pan, Aegle, Silvanus, Aurora, the Dew, satyrs, pans and aigipans, and six varieties of nymphs and personifications of the winter and spring, of the months of March, April and May and of the winds Boreas, Auster and Zephyrus all appear in the company of conventional shepherds. It should be noted that in spite of this conglomeration of figures the description is unhurried and dreamy, a little masterpiece of the early sixteenth century.

4. MICROCOSM AND MACROCOSM

At two points of his literary career Lemaire de Belges reaches his climax with regard to literary imagery. This happens in the second letter of the *Epîtres de l'amant vert* and the chapters dealing with the marriage of Peleus and Tethis in the *Illustrations de Gaule et singularités de Troie* (I, 203-239). The difference between he two descriptions lies in the esthetic concept they impart. The first re-presents the universe in a nutshell. It is a miniature full of variety and suggestive of large spatial expanse in spite of its delicate design. In the second the author, inspired by the magnitude of his model, reaches out for the endless with restless lines and powerful strokes.

The epistles of the green lover are both poetic and facetious. In them Lemaire makes a parrot write letters to his patron, Margaret of Austria. A favorite bird of the princess, this parrot was swallowed during a trip of hers by a dog and its loss was bewailed by its owner after her return. The poet imagined that unable to bear the absence of its mistress the bird committed suicide by jumping into the mouth of the dog. Before doing so he wrote a farewell letter to her, expressing in the style of courtly love, his affection. His success with this whim-sical idea prompted Lemaire to compose a second letter supposed to have been written from beyond the tomb. In it the parrot describes to Margaret his trip in animal hell and animal heaven. It is this second letter we here will analyze.

It depicts a biblio-mythological cosmos all equipped with earth, hell and heaven. And it contains Ovidean and Dantean motifs and elements of Celtic legend. [122] Since the central character is a bird, the

---

[122] Jean Lemaire de Belges, *Les épîtres de l'amant vert*, ed. Jean Frappier (Paris, 1948), XXXII. All parenthetical references pertaining to the work relate to this edition.

flying figure of Mercury is aptly chosen as a guide for the spiritual journey through the three regions. The god and the parrot fly first horizontally along the surface of the earth, then vertically down to the depth of Hades, and finally they climb up to the Elysian fields.

The spatial effects of the little work are successfully introduced by the flight of the two figures to Hades:

> Print mon esprit, tout innocent et vierge,
> Puis, en volant plus legier que le vent,
> Me mena vœir le tenebreux convent
> Des infernaulx.
>
> (vss. 60-63, p. 20)

The distance flown is considerable. It evidently led from the castle of Pont d'Ain in Savoie where the parrot died to the cave of Taenarum in the Peloponnese as indicated by the author who fixed the location of the entry to Hades in accordance with a tradition perpetuated by Virgil and Ovid. [123] The description of the descent to hell is effective:

> Droit là voit on ung grant trou tartaricque,
> Si treshideux que nulle rhetoricque
> Ne sçauroit bien sa laideur exprimer:
> Au fons duquel alasmes abismer
> Mercure et moy.
>
> (vss. 69-73, p. 20)

The verb *abismer* and the phrase *grant trou tartaricque* impress upon the reader the profundity of the hollow. Tartarus, a gaping hole, was supposed to be equidistant between the firmament and the surface of the earth. The trip to heaven is based on magic, with no immediate appeal to the senses. After the god and the parrot drink from Lethe, the river of oblivion, they climb up a narrow and straight road to a region whose height is immeasurable, since it materializes in the realm of metaphysics. The author calls it *les haulx lieux soubverains* (vs. 282, p. 27). In approaching this heaven, only a pure and immaterial light is discernible. Lemaire's idea of the bird paradise is inspired by Ovid, Virgil, [124] Dante and by medieval tales on the voyage of Saint Brendan.

---

[123] Vergil, *Georgics*, IV, 465 and Ovid, *Metamorphoses*, X, 13.

[124] *Aeneid*, VI, 703-715 and 748-751 and 893-896.

Purgatorio, XXXI, 94-105. C. Wahlund, *Die altfranzösische Prosaübersetzung von Brendans Meerfahrt* (Upsala, 1900).

From the latter, Lemaire borrowed the light effects as well as the location of the paradise in an *insula deliciosa*. [125] Yet the panorama has originality and is bigger and brighter than anything found in its medieval counterpart. The bird's-eye view of a big island in a glittering ocean belongs by its excellent visibility and large spatial effects to the Renaissance:

> Et regarday la grand mer spacïeuse
> Qui circuÿt l'isle delicïeuse.
> Tranquille estoit et calme la marine,
> Clere et luisant comme belle verrine,
> L'isle eslevée ou milieu, grande et lée,
> Ayant maint tertre et umbreuse valée.
>
> (vss. 327-332, p. 29)

At Mercury's departure from the parrot, the author evokes once again the haunting image of flight:

> Puis il s'en vole, et m'apperent ses trasses
> Par le chemin de l'air qu'il trenche et fend,
> Dont nulle riens ne l'empesche ou deffend.
>
> (vss. 314-316, p. 28)

The verbs *trancher* and *fendre* give corporeality to the air and make it palpable to the senses.

Passion for variety leads here to encyclopedic enumerations of a picturesque sort often found in the French Renaissance. An overwhelming number of brids, fish, insects, four-legged beasts and monsters populate hell and heaven. In some cases the text refers to specific animals barrowed from mythological or historical accounts, from hagiography and from the Bible. Other passages refer to species. The animals belong to hell or heaven according to a moral evaluation of their acts, their natural traits, or their general appeal. Based as it is on documentation, the material the author was able to find causes him not only scholarly delight but also astounds him with the diversity of phenomena history and life can offer to the eye. By the multitude of objects he has gathered together, Lemaire once again anticipates

---

[125] "Invenitque insulam juxta montem lapidis, nomine insulam deliciosam." *Nagigatio Sancti Brendani Abbatis,* ed. Carl Selmer (Notre Dame, 1959), 18-19, p. 4.

Rabelais, although he is softer, less rapid, less impetuous. By the virtuosity and unexpectedness of his findings he also predicts certain passages in Montaigne, such as the latter's enumeration of men who died while engaged in sexual intercourse. No less than 64 particular animals or species are placed into hell and 57 into heaven, and to the latter should be added a vision of "thousands" of birds that perched on the green orange tree where the parrot-protagonist had settled. The following partial list of "hellish" animals will give an idea of the colorful description: Cerberus, the seven-headed hydra, the bulls Jason defeated, the bull that was Pasophaë's lover, Saint George's dragon, the dragon that threatened to swallow Saint Margaret, the raven that did return to Noah's arch, the Minotaur, the serpent that bit Eurydice, the horses that quartered Saint Hippolytus, the ones that tore apart Hippolytus, son of Theseus, the horse that threw and killed John II Prince of Portugal, the man-eating horses of Diomedes, the horse that threw and killed Mary of Burgundy, the mule whose hoof served to keep the poison by which Alexander the Great was killed, the wildboar that killed Adonis, the pig on which the horse of Philip, son of King Louis VI. stumbled causing the death of the prince, the dogs that tore Actaeon apart transformed by Diana into a stag, the dog that ate the parrot described in the tale, and the sea monster that wanted to swallow Andromeda- (vss. 75-189, pp. 20-24).

The momentum of the description varies. In heaven the poetic and dreamy mood requires a slowing down of the narration. The description of single events occasionally extends into three or four verses. At other points the pace is more fluent and one half or one full verse suffices most of the time to portray a bird or an animal:

> Faisans bien painctz, pellicans solitaires,
> Simples coulons, arondes salutaires,
> Rossignoletz doulx et melodïeux
> Et chardonnetz d'aprendre estudïeux,
> Cocqz liberaulx, hardiz et diligens,
> Serins, tarins, qui sont plaisans et gens
> Merles faictiz, gelinettes utilles
> Cignes tous blancz, aloëtes gentilles,
> Grues veillans à leurs tours ordinaires,
> Aigles royaulx, cicoignes debonnaires,
> Et autres cent especes d'oiseletz
> Tous vertueux, joliz et genteletz.

(vss. 397-408, p. 31)

The marriage of Peleus and Thetis in the *Illustrations* is a whirl-wind of shapes and figures (I, pp. 203-230). [126] At first the story shows the gathering of the gods (I, pp. 203-212) then the wedding itself (I, pp. 213-220) and finally, after the intervention of Discordia, the flight of Juno, Venus, and Pallas with Mercury in the lead to the Troad to seek the judgment of Paris (I, 221-230).

From the point of view of spatial representation two main motifs can be distinguished in these chapters. There are two-dimensional images imposed on the surface of the earth. Others are vertical or three-dimensional altogether and move about in every sense, from the sky to the bottom of the earth. Among the latter three particular varieties can be observed. Some of the gods described associate with phenomena through their exterior and their function in nature. Some other objects radiate into space, and again others evoke it through flight.

In the horizontal sense Lemaire presents a picture of the Me-diterranean, its surrounding lands and its islands. As pointed out before, the image of this region has been developing little by little from the beginning of the work. Suddenly now the sea appears in a single scene in its entity, an esthetically conceived summary of all that went ahead. The geographical facts come into view as classical deities appear in different localities and move towards Thessaly. Tethys, the goddess of the ocean — not to be confused with Thetis the bride who is a mere nymph — enters the Mediterranean at Gibraltar mounted on a chariot driven by a whale and surrounded by feminine figures most of whom swim in the water. Since she reigns over all the earth, her appearance permits the author to give a global view of the ocean even before unfolding the image of the Mediterranean: "Le grand Océan, qui va et vient, flotte et reflotte deux fois le iour" (I, 205). The rest of the gods come from the cities, states, straights, peninsulas and islands of the Mediterranean, and as they move along, the places identified with each of them seem to light up one by one. Eolus comes from the Lipari Islands north of Sicily, Vulcan from Lemnos, Diana from Crete, Phoebus from Rhodes, Venus from Cy-prus, Neptune from Tenedos. Moving eastward we now arrive in Asia

---

[126] The less voluminous, more earthbound and restrained treatment of the theme by Catullus (LXIV) clearly conveys the difference between Roman and Renaissance imagery.

Minor. Cybele comes from Phrygia, and Priapus, the god of the gardens, from Lampsacus in the Dardanelles. [127] In a whimsical pattern the author takes us once more back west. Hercules, Faunus, and Silvanus come from Tibur, today's Tivoli in Italy, and Ceres comes from Sicily. And then the territory of Greece itself makes its appearance. Pluto leaves Molossia, one of the mythological entrances to Hades, locatted in Epirus. Juno departs from Mycenae, Pan from Arcadia, Pallas from Athens, Mars from Thracia, and Bacchus, Silenus and their companions from Thebes. With the appearance of Neptune we return once more to the image of the sea, and since we now are in the midst of the Mediterranean, the water is seen in its relation to land. The gods inside and outside of Neptune's chariot denote: "la circuition que la mer fait alentour de la terre" (I, 207). Also in the retinue are Tritons who blow into sea shells, symbolizing the noise the sea makes when hitting against the shores: "Et menoit avec luy ses instrumentaires et precurseurs appelez Tritons qui cornent en bussines de coquilles de mer, et designent le bruit que la mer fait contre les rivages et rochers" (I, 207). The landscape is also composed of smaller territorial formations that materialize in their relationships to the gods: Priapus evokes gardens (I, 208), Ceres wheatfields (I, 208-209), Bacchus, Silenus, and Marsyas vineyards (I, p. 208), Founus and Silvanus groves (I, p. 208), Pan pastures (I, p. 209), Flora flowering lands (I, p. 206), and Venus blooming orchards (I, p. 207).

The three-dimensional realities evolve simultaneously. At the beginning of the tale the entire universe appears for a moment. Jupiter, says the author, called together the gods of the sky, the sea and the earth. Then most remote spots of the world appear, the highest on the sky and the lowest in the depth of the earth (I, p. 203). Because of the great distance the deities that dwell in these regions cannot attend the wedding. Saturnus must stay in the sky and Demogorgon is entombed, as it were, in the depth of the earth: "Le vieillard Saturne, triste, melancolique, et tardif, selon la nature de sa planette: Lequel sexcusa de venir, pource quil estoit malade. Et aussi que sa sphere et region est trop loingtaine de la terre habitable. Pareillement lancien pere des Dieux Demogorgon demoura en son abyme, et au parfond centre de la terre: si nen peut onques eschapper" (I, pp. 204-205).

---

[127] According to Lemaire in the Propontis, i.e. the Sea of Marmora: one of several geographical errors in the text.

The cosmic melancholia expressed in these lines is rather interesting, and perhaps rare in a Christian author. The notion of spirits placed at the two extremities of the world makes us shudder. Other gods who dwell far from the surface of the earth partake of the wedding ceremony just the same. Tethys and her companions emerge from the depth of the sea: "Et toutes estoient sorties de leurs parfons gouffres et repaires de mer" (I, 205). Pluto comes "de basse terre" (I, 209) from Dis, the Roman version of Hades, whose depth can be measured by the darkness of the horses that pull his chariot: "Chevaux plus noirs que meure" (I, 209). [128]

The divinities that live in cities and islands and contribute as we have seen, through their earthly voyage to the horizontal aspect of the tableau, also imply three-dimensional phenomena, since they reside simultaneously in their natural habitat in the cosmos. Lemaire who derived this concept of the duality of the divine presence, as he himself states, from his readings in Vergil and Boccaccio (I, 205) has Diana, Aurora, and Apollo walk behind each other on the ground while making them appear at the same time in space as actors in a spectacular celestial drama, the change from night to day. Diana, the goddess of the moon, who wears a crescent on her head, describes by means of symbolic objects that surround her, her course in the sky. The two wheels of her chariot and the black and white horse that drive it stand for the two cycles of the moon, the one completed at night, the other by day (I, 206). That the scene here described actually takes place on the firmament is most clearly shown by the next figure, Aurora the dawn, who walks behind Diana "removing all nightly darkness before her" (I, 207). And then comes Apollo, the sun, who in his brilliant chariot "circles constantly around the earth (I, 207). According to signs of the zodiac, the irradiant diadem on his head is adorned with twelve precious stones, while the decoration of his chariot reflects the light of the sun: diamonds, chrosolites, rubies and other jewels enrich the guilded wheels, the silvery spokes and the pole made of solid gold (I, 206).

---

[128] *mûre* could be the fruit of the black mulberry or of the blackberry (mûre sauvage, mûre de ronce, mûre de haie). The black mulberry (morus nigra) known to the Middle Ages, was superseded since then by the Morus Alba that has a purplish-black fruit. The blackberry is of a different family altogether.

Whereas the above mentioned gods enact mere episodes in the universe the god Pan depicts the whole of nature by his appearance. His horn stands for the crescent of the moon, his red flaming face for the sun, his long beard for the elements that descend down to earth. His shoulders adorned with a multicolored hide represents the star-studded sky, his heavy and hairy legs the surface of the earth. The seven tubes of his pipe are tuned to seven planets (I, 219).

Spatial effects of a different kind are brought about by the effusion of light and sound. Light emanates from Jupiter who is seen seated on a throne on top of Mount Pelion that is of considerable height in itself. This light has the brightness of the planet Jupiter and illuminates the heavens (p. 213). Emanations of sound materialize on a smaller scale. The music made by Pan's pipe can be heard throughout the valleys of Thessaly, the author says, and Echo the nymph responds to it (I, 219-220). The reverberation of sound in space has magic. It arouses in us a vague feeling of unlimited expanse, a feeling of the infinite.

There are three flight scenes in these chapters, each of which becomes an interesting serial adventure. The first one, at the beginning of the tale, shows Mercury fluttering about the whole universe: "Mercure sen coula parmy la region aërine clere et sapphirine, pour parfournir son message, lequel il acheva en peu dheure, combien que les personnages susquelz il saddressoit feissent residence en diverses pars, de gran distance et remotion" (I, 204). It is a fine passage that conveys the extension and speed of the god's trip and the coloring and clarity of the air.

The second flight is more colorful and sinister (I, 222). It contains visual antitheses. It deals with the goddess "Discordia" — a Roman version of Eris — who feels insulted for not having been invited to the wedding, and, seeking revenge, brings about a quarrel between Juno, Venus, and Pallas. She flings towards the goddesses a golden apple which she brought from the garden of the Hesperides and which is to be given to the most beautiful of the three. The dragonlike shape and the brown wings of the deity, a dark spot floating in the air, make the scene somber and ominous. The length of her aerial voyage is enormous in a mythical sense for, according to Greek legend, the garden of the Hesperides is at the spot where the sun sinks into the sea, a point whose location is remote and undefinable. Impressive also is the arrival of the goddess in Thessaly. She flies to the top of Mount Pelion, squats down in the deadly shadow of a yew tree and makes herself invisible. Her sudden disappearance makes her flight through contrast all the more conspicuous. Her last motion through space is short and quick and leads to the depth of the earth. As if shot from a cross-bow she speeds down to hell: "elle senfuyt plus vite quun carreau darbaletre, et salla plonger au fin fons d'Enfer, là ou est son domicile" (I, 222).

The flight to the Troad by the three goddesses and by Mercury, who thereby makes his second appearance in the story, is a splendid piece of writing and a satisfactory conclusion to these outstanding chapters of Lemaire's work (I, 226-227). Once more colorful spots appear in the sky. Juno's chariot is flown by peacocks, Venus' by swans or doves. Both goddesses have a large retinue in their respective vehicles. Pallas, who is all by herself, has wings adjusted to her arms and flies in solitary grandeur. There is a fine airy quality in the description of her voyage: "Quand donques toutes les trois Deesses furent prestes at attintees, [129] chacune sesleva de terre, et se meirent en la voye parmy lair spacieux et cler, suivans le noble Dieu Mercure qui les precedoit, et trenchoit devant elles la region azuree, plus viste que nul aigle Royal ne fait quand il voit sa proye. Le Roy Jupiter et tous les autres Dieux et Deesses les convoyerent des yeux tant quilz les peurent choisir" (I, 226-227). The combination of verb and adjective in "trenchoit . . . la region azuree," is interesting for the blue of the air which conveys immateriality contrasts with the image of its being "sliced" and thereby interprets the mystery of flight, the motion of a solid body moving through what appears to be empty space. Stirring also is the disappearance of the group before the eyes of those left behind. The opposition between a spectacular object and the sense of nothingness here is even more impressive than in the story of Discordia, for the flying figures now are swallowed by never-ending space.

In addition to the image of aerial magnitude the author also points out geographical expanse. The trip passes over Thessaly, Macedonia, Thracia and the Hellespont to its destination, the Troad. [130]

---

[129] accomodées.

[130] The Cyclades and some other islands the author thinks are in the Hellespont (Dardanelles) are elsewhere. He also believes that certain islands belong to the Cyclades that are outside of it. Let us observe finally that the

Interesting in the presentation of the flight is the everchanging position of the observer. At the beginning the travelers were viewed from the ground. They took off and disappeared in a distance. Shortly thereafter the author is in the air and looks down with the gods to the earth below. Towards the end of the journey he is once more on the ground and sees the gods descend. Their orderly formation reminds him of cranes. At the last moment he once again moves up into space. While viewing the earth in the company of Mercury, he spots Paris in the fields and has the god drop down to the ground with the speed of lightning (I, 229). With this abrupt act the mythological voyage is over.

The sources for multitudinousness and variety in the marriage of Peleus and Thetis (I, 203-279) come almost exclusively from classical antiquity. Monogenic as the description may be, the geographical facts and the mythological figures are more numerous and motley than anywhere else. In the chapter dealing with the gathering of the gods no less than 32 cities, states, provinces, continents, islands, peninsulas, straights, seas and mountains are mentioned around the Mediterranean. About 100 gods or demigods and 40 animals are identified by name or species. Yet the author intimates that he could do better: "Oultre les dessusdits, plusieurs autres Dieux et Deesses, Demydieux, Demydeesses, Heroës et Heroïdes, [131] toutes pars arriverent à la feste, dont le nombre est presques Innumerable" (I, 211). The number is matched by diversity and richness. Eight chariots appear on land and on sea, each heavily decorated, pulled by different animals and surrounded by a colorful cortege. Tethys' chariot is pulled by whales, Diana's by stags and horses, Neptune's by twelve walrusses, Cybele's by two tamed lions, Pluto's by three black horses, Mars' by horses of a hideous color, covered by foam and blood, Bacchus' by lynxes and tigers, Appolo's by four horses, Silenus rides on a donkey (I, 216). Other gods walk, and some like Eolus may be considered as wandering along in the air. A crowd of half-deities, moving about the main ones, some calmly, some impassioned, add to the general commotion. Around Tethys are her daughter Doris, and Sirens and nymphs and

---

names of a number of islands here mentioned are today unknown or misspelled beyond recognition. Their identification would require laborious search in Lemaire's source material.

[131] Heroïnes.

Nereïds who ride on dolphins. Tritons can be seen next to Neptune, and next to Cybele Corybantes who are armed and carry cudgels and sound dulciners and drums and kettledrums. Diana is accompanied by nymphs, Pluto has brought along Proserpine, Mars is being washed and disarmed by women. And Silenus who is drunk is held on his donkey by Marsyas and his companions. With Eolus has come Zephyrus and his wife Flora, with Vulcan two giants, with Venus Cupido, Voluptuousness and the three Graces, with Pallas the nine Muses and their mother Mnemosyne.

Often, anomalous or monstrous exteriors add to the variety of the scene. Centaurs, giants, satyrs, furies, lame Vulcan, three-headed Cerberus, two-faced Janus were not as commonplace in the early sixteenth century as they were later, and the punctiliousness of the description shows that the author felt he had to familiarize his readers with their peculiarities. Symbolic outfits and dresses also make for variety. Mercury wears a hood with feathers, has wings on his heels, and holds a rod adorned with twisted figures of snakes in his hand. Vesta's apparel is full of flowers and verdure. Cybele has a royal scepter in her hand, wears a crown ornamented with towers, cities and castles and a dress covered with the picture of forests, grass and shrubs. Bacchus is naked, has his head covered with ivy, and wears a shoot for a scepter.

There is diversity of a different sort in the wedding scene itself (I, 213-220). It is manifest above all in a colorful landscape whose richness is made all the more startling since it bursts forth suddenly from a barren ground. Gods and goddesses cover the empty earth with grass, flowers, dew, fountains, shrubbery and trees: "Flora, la gracieuse Nymphe ... sentremit de tapisser la noble montaigne de fresche verdure, et de plantes aromatiques et flairans violettes dyaprees de maintes couleurs, dont son mary le gentil Zephyrus ... lui faisoit fourniture" (I, 215). The passage recalls vaguely the fifteenth century pastorals except for the excess of detail. Twenty-five varieties of flowers and 14 varieties of shrubs are mentioned (I, 215).

At the wedding festivities the image remains motley, although the rhythm is not the same. The cadence is slower, and the description becomes almost static. Most of the gods have a task at the preparation and the serving of the banquet, and they form a grotesque and varied ensemble. The giants, Brontes and Pyracmon, keep the kitchen fire going. Priapus, the god of the gardens, is in charge of greenery and the sauces and Vulcan of the buffet. Perseus and Jason are carvers, Hebe and Ganymede cup-bearers. Ceres, the goddess of wheat, provides for the needs of the pantry. The companions of Bacchus furnish the wine, Pomona and Frutesea, the fruit. Hymenaeus, the god of weddings, is the maître d'hôtel. The Tritons blow water, the satyrs serve the meat given to them by Chiron the centaur who is the head cook for the occasion.

The last scene, the flight of Mercury and the goddesses (I, 226-230) presents once more variety in motion. While the number of deities here is smaller, the fact that masses of mythological individuals are crowded into the flying chariots creates an impression of multitudinousness. With Venus and Juno fly Hebe, 14 nymphs, Iris, the three graces, Voluptusousness, Cupido and Psyche.

Lemaire's imagery does not have the brilliance of those found in the great sixteenth century French authors. He does not have the bulkiness and materiality of Rabelais or the magnificence of Ronsard. Inasmuch as he undergoes fifteenth-century influences he has some of the medieval intimacy of Christine de Pisan or of René d'Anjou. A transitional poet, he combines the Middle Ages with the Renaissance, and his work has a beauty all its own.

CHAPTER III

RABELAIS

In the history of the French Renaissance Rabelais takes a place
of his own. [132] Multitude, diversity and spatial grandeur turn into
enormousness in his work. This is a special version of the Renaissance frame of mind, a superlative of its aspirations. Traces of enormousness can be found in Lemaire de Belges, who deals with giants
in his *Illustrations*. It becomes in Rabelais a literary genre, as it did in
Folengo's *Opus Macaronicum*, in Pulci's *Morgante Maggiore* and in the
Grandes Chroniques, all of which served as models to our author. [133]

Variety and grandeur are twin expressions of the same principle
in Rabelais. The first is a constant, restless drive towards the immense, the second the full materialization of that drive in powerful
single images. On the one hand the author piles up pictures into big
heaps or even comparatively small ones that, nevertheless, through
their presentation, reveal the general trend towards the enormous.
On the other hand, Rabelais creates vast images, not only of the
giants themselves but also of natural phenomena, large sections of
land and sea, and sometimes of the cosmos. In a small number of passages, finally, both diversity and grandeur attain a sedate sort of
harmony: they add up to a well-rounded ensemble of visual effects
that enchant the eye. Rabelais turns here into an artist.

---

[132] His characteristics as a Renaissance author have been marred by an
exaggerated stress on the medieval aspects of his thought: Wallace K. Ferguson, *The Renaissance in Historical Thought* (Boston, 1948), pp. 352-354.
[133] Jean Plattard, *La vie et l'œuvre de Rabelais* (Paris, 1939), pp. 142-
151.

The opening lines of *Pantagruel,* known to have been the first of all the books in the order of composition, [134] reproduce fully the two main motives (*Pant.,* i, pp. 171-174). [135] As is so often the case with great literary works, the author expresses his intentions at the outset describing the genesis of giantism on earth. Spatial grandeur materializes first in the image of the cosmos; in the figure of the giants grandeur mingles with variety. The author's universe is a farcical astrological tableau. Absurd irregularities in the calender associate with strange events in the sky. The sun stumbles slightly to the left like a bow-legged man, the moon varies its course by five fathoms, and some of the fixed stars change their position through the general vibration of the firmament: "Tellement que la Pléiade moyenne laissant ses compaignons, déclina vers l'Equinoctial, et l'estoille nommé l'Espy laissa la Vierge, se retirant vers la Balance" (*Pant.,* i, p. 172). At the same time unusual occurences set in on earth. We are in biblical times, the period of the first fratiricide. Imbued with the blood of Abel, the earth becomes excessively rich and fertile. Especially big are the medlars grown in that year, and those who eat them become monstruous in a variety of ways. Some grow excessively in parts of their body — their bellies, their shoulders, their noses, their ears, their legs, etc. Some turn into giants altogether. Thanks to supernatural circumstances, variety and grandeur grow simultaneously out of the enriched earth in the figures of the many-shaped giants.

Variety is not always found in conjunction with grandeur. It is a vast subject that because of its complexities can hardly be discussed summarily, except perhaps if we relate it to its sources, each of which yields a torrent of material. Outstanding among them, of course, is learning, most characteristically such learning as bears upon time and space: antique and Christian history, mythology, the Bible, folklore, geography and astronomy are of outstanding importance. These combine with zoology, botany, physiology, biology, medicine. Among the arts philosophy, ethics, architecture, painting, music and languages play a rather prominent part. The primarily bookish sources go hand in hand with facts deriving from the observation of contemporary

---

[134] *Pantagruel,* ed. Verdun Saulnier (Paris, 1946), IX.

[135] Rabelais, *Œuvres complètes* (Paris: Bibliothèque de la Pléiade, 1955), pp. 193-199. All parenthetical references found in the text relate to this edition.

life. The occupations are for Rabelais an arsenal of information. Industries, the crafts and commerce, agriculture, warfare, travel, inventions, ecclesiastical and university life are on the top of the list. Simple observations made on life, on human behavior, on human types and events and on the phenomena of nature further enrich the list.

Variety as manifest in single passages is enhanced by the mingling of heterogeneous realities. Floods of images bursting forth from often unrelated pools of thought merge and eddy, forming a multicolored and often contrasting whole. In Epistemon's vision of hell (*Pant.*, xxx, pp. 294-302) which shows great men of the past engaged in lowly occupations, contemporary conditions flow together with the past. Rabelais presents no less than 88 sixteenth century professions and applies them to individuals taken from Greek and Roman history, mythology and legend, as well as from French literature, folklore and history. Let us observe that the author's mood often changes in addition to the changing subject within a description. In the first four paragraphs of the chapter that deals with Gargamelle's condition before she gives birth to Gargantua the tone is in turns learned, rustic, obscene and popular, while the theme, as the discussion moves along, touches on physiology, agriculture, the Church, the medieval theater, medicine and the French provinces (*Garg*, iv, pp. 14-15).

The processing and organization of this tremendous body of material is one of the interesting problems to consider in the work of Rabelais. Nothing is further removed from the truth than the oft repeated criticism on the encyclopedic character of his style. [136] The unrestrained gusto with which he absorbs facts and the effervescence with which he renders them differs essentially from any scholarly or pedantic bearing.

This zest is evident in the very genesis of the scenes, the creative process that propels the Rabelaisian composition. It assumes two typical forms: it can be either proliferous or accumulative. In the first case it is the result of mere visual impulses. The starting point then is a single object that produces related ones by association. As they add up to an often enormous sequence, they develop from one another, produce each other, as it were, on the spur of the moment

---

[136] Jean Plattard, *La vie et l'œuvre de Rabelais*, p. 92.

and often with great speed. The phenomena seem to double by an innate force, like cells. In other cases the author gathers living material from all over to put it into a common caldron where the items boil and whirl about and melt together forming a tumultuous whole.

An example of the proliferous process is a grotesque visual game inserted into the study of the war on the island Farouche between Pantagruel and his followers on the one hand and the chitterlings on the other (IV, xxxviii, pp. 643-644). In a bold flight of fancy, the author creates the notion that sausages enter into the composition of some outstanding human beings, animals and divinities. The *andouilles* thereby are identified metaphorically, undoubtedly beacause of their shape, with serpents, fishes and phalli. One image seem to grow out of another. The giants who fought the gods from Mount Pelion were serpents in half of their body, therefore chitterlings, says Rabelais. Next, he introduces the biblical serpent, a sausage in its whole body. This gives him an opportunity to move on to the phallus. Basing his observation on a statement probably found in H. C. Agrippa's *De originali peccato* he observes that the tempter of Adam and Eve was ithyphallic. This leads to the figure of Priapus, who as a god of gardens — the Greek equivalent of the garden of Eden — and as a "tempter of women" is associated in Rabelais's interpretation with the serpent and was transformed according to mythological accounts into a phallus. Still adhering to the image of serpents the author now mentions the Himantopodes or thong-legged ones, a nation that once lived in Ethiopia and moved along with a serpentine crawling kind of gait according to Pliny. [137] The commentary now shifts from the serpent to the fish, to water nymphs with fishtails, the Breton Melusina and the Scythian Ora. To the same species belongs also Erichtonius, who invented the coach, the litter and the chariot in order to hide his legs in these vehicles. Besides physical features, the individual character traits correspond to sausages as well. From the facetious idea that chitterlings are courageous develops, with no visual interpretation, one single image, that of the Swiss as a nation, who because of their bravery may have been sausages, Rabelais says.

In the opposite process, the cumulative from of composition, in which the author assembles facts that fit a visually undefined or

---

[137] *Natural History*, V, 8.

vaguely defined thematic abstraction, variety is even more apparent than in the case of proliferation. In a description of unusual deaths (IV, xvii, pp. 589-590) a general topic with no discernible model as a starting point, turns into concrete images that are vastly different from one another. Aeschylus has been killed by the impact of the fall of a turtle dropped by a high flying eagle. Startling are the possibilities of strangulation. Anacreon was strangled by the kernel of a grape, Faebius, a Roman praetor, by the hair of a goat found in a bowl of milk. One individual died from an effort to hold back letting air, another from the bite of a cat on his little finger and again another from having punctured his pulse with a needle. The removal of a mite from the skin with a penknife, laughing at the sight of a donkey eating figs, sucking in a soft-boiled egg, picking one's teeth with a sage-stalk, paying a debt, laughing at one's own painting of a dead woman, eating butter at the mouth of a hot oven have all been causing the death of people.

Eevery fine literary creation has characteristics of a living organism in which parts reflect the whole in their texture and in their essence. The above-mentioned two modes of composition are not only manifest in individual scenes but also in large sections of the work.

Proliferation is the process by which the images of giants grow out of each other in *Gargantua*. Earlier drawings seem to be echoed by later ones in typical incidents that depict either the inner organs or the exterior of the individuals. Food, drink and procreation are some of the recurrent motives. In farcically vulgar passages Grandgousier's and Gargamelle's eating habits match each other (iii; p. 12, iv, pp. 14-16; vi, pp. 22-23), and the unusual 11 months pregnancy of Gargamelle corresponds to her giving birth to Gargantua through her left ear (iii, p. 13; vi, p. 23). In the same way reference to Gargantua's big throat at his birth and the fact that he demanded to drink as soon as he opened his mouth leads up to the episode in which he washes down towards his throat with a torrent of red wine the pilgrims he had swallowed (vii, p. 25; viii, pp. 111-113). There also is a strong affinity between incidents that show the normal world side by side with the giants. The scene in which Gargantua drowns the Parisians in his urine, removes the bells of Notre Dame (xvii, p. 54), mistakes the cannon balls shot at him for flies (xxxvi, p. 107), destroys a fortress with a tree he had pulled out of the ground (xxxvi, pp. 107-108), and combs cannon balls out of his hair (xxxvii, pp. 109-110) are related to one another in this respect.

In contrast the organization of the *Tiers Livre* follows the cumulative pattern. Single happenings here do not emanate from preceding ones, but are inserted into a general scheme and thereby connected without borrowing each others' feautures. The consultation of all sorts of individuals in matters of Panurge's marriage being the moving power of the plot leads to a large number of colorful encounters whose only link is the topic. Indeed there is no common pictorial denominator to the bookish atmosphere of the Virgilian lottery (xii, pp. 366-370), the mystifying mood of Panurge's dream (xiv, pp. 376-380), or the noisy and vulgar character of the visit with the Sibyl of Panzoust (xvii, pp. 387-390), to mention only the first three of the twelve parleys, all of which develop their graphic characteristics along their own line.

After their genesis the zest and animation of the images depends on their rhythm, the momentum that connects them to form a stirring visual emsemble. This aspect of the composition depends on the mood of the author. Sometimes the description unrolls with breathtaking speed by means of single nouns, adjectives or verbs. In this flood of words individual items are not easily discernible but create an impression of great abundance. Sometimes, when the supply that serves to feed the subject matter seems exhausted, the author opens another sluice whence will gush forth with the same acceleration a new brand of forms and colors. At the outset of Gargantua, in the oft discussed description of silenes, an enumeration of the exterior of boxes is followed by a list of objects found inside: "Silènes estoient... pinctes au-dessus de figures joyeuses et frivoles, comme de harpies, satyres, oysons bridéz, lièvres cornuz, canes bastées, boucqs volans, cerfz limonniers et aultres telles pinctures... mais au dedans l'on réservait les fines drogues comme baulme, ambre gris, amomon, musc, zivette, pierreries et aultres choses précieuses" (*Garg.*, Prologue de l'auteur, p. 3). [138] Variety is offered in two keys, as it were, with contrasts between form and content.

---

[138] This theme often is used by humanists and has its origin in Plato's *Symposium*, 215 A. The contrast between Plato's well-balanced simplicity and Rabelais's volubility as apparent in the passages here in question, could be used as a starting point for a study comparing Greek and Renaissance imagery.

This most "staccato" form of expression sometimes gives room to a somewhat broader treatment containing pictures that emerge from phrases and short scentences. The tableau as a whole still is fractured, but the single parts are somewhat more voluminous and more easily grasped. Otherwise they equal simple enumerations in size and variability. An example is the scene that shows Frère Jean hitting about with a processional cross among Picrochole's soldiers. Rabelais the doctor here indulges in a display of human anatomy. The soldiers are attacked in their heads, their arms and legs, their vertebrae, loins, noses, eyes, jaws, teeth, shoulder blades, the shins, hips, forebones, etc. A selection of colorful verbs serves to enliven the substantives and make them stand out: crush, break, dislocate, strike down, unjoint, bruise, split, kick in, cut up, blaken with blows, remove, cut to pieces are some of the verbs used (*Garg.*, xxvii, p. 85). [139]

There is an even larger and smoother medium in which the single elements of the series connect in a fluent discussion. The feminine and masculine uniforms of the Thelemites, a splendid account of contemporary fashion, are described in such a manner (*Garg.*, lvi, pp. 156-159). [140]

Sometimes diversity is worked into a broad composition. Instead of being heaped on one another, the parts are organized and grouped into thematic units. Although the quantity often is tremendous, the pace here is more temperate, and the general tone less impetuous and impatient. Such is the passage in which Dindenault praises his sheep to Panurge (IV, vi, vii, p. 554-559). As a reproduction of popular mannerisms, the patter of the tradesman does not come forth hastily but in the slow and persuasuve manner used in bargaining. The pictures create each other in a comfortable thought process: "De la toison de ces moutons seront faictz les fins draps de Rouen; les louschetz des balles de Limestre, au pris d'elle, ne sont que bourre. De la peau seront faictz les beaulz marroquins, lesquelz on vendra pour marroquins turquins, ou de Montélimart, ou de Hespaigne pour le pire. Des boyeaulx on fera chordes de violons et harpes, lesquelles tant chèrement on vendra comme si feussent chordes de Munican ou

---

[139] Similar in its effect is the scene in which a Turkish pasha kills another Turk with a spit in a tall tale of Panurge (*Pant.*, XVI).

[140] Less picturesque but similar in presentation is an enumeration of Panurge's trick instruments (*Pant.*, XVI).

Aquileie" (IV, vi, p. 556). An attractive change now occurs in the melody of the passage. With no modification of the tempo, animation sets in through the rise of the tone. While the phrases retain their comfortable and even rhythm, the mood becomes more sprightly because the discourse has moved from reality into a world of fancy. The new tone is introduced by the slightly exalted reference to violins and harps in the above quotation. At this point Panurge shows some money to the tradesman, who, inspired by the spectacle, abandons himself to his imagination: his animals are of the race of the sheep with the golden fleece; they come from the country where hogs eat myrobolans, and sows feed on the flowers of orange trees; wonder drugs are made of their manure, and their horns, if buried in the ground by daylight, bring forth the best asparagus. Every bone, every part of the inside of the sheep is a miracle in its own right (IV, vii, pp. 556-558).

For a fuller treatment of Rabelaisian esthetics we shall add to the pictorial effects dependent on genesis and rhythm those that derive from an interplay between series of single images with static or dynamic characteristics. Some are motionless and dazzle the eye as they appear and disappear, integrating into a complex whole of forms and colors. Such is the enumeration of dead animals that succumbed to the earth devastating fraught prior to Pantagruel's birth (*Pant.*, ii, p. 178), or the description of a large group of monks whom Pantagruel and his associates met on the high seas on the trip they took in search of the *Dive Bouteille*: "Jacobins, Jésuites, Capussins, Hermites, Augustins, Bernardins, Célestins, Théatins, Egnatins, Amadéans, Cordeliers, Carmes, Minimes et aultres saintz religieux" (IV, xviii, p. 591). Different is the impression we get from pictures that are in motion. Their quick succession creates an odd and complex tableau, particularly if executed by a single person or object that does not change much its place and fills a restricted area with a multitude of contortions. Such is the sensation we get from the chapter in which little Gargantua goes with a wooden horse through every possible act of horsemanship (*Garg.*, xii, pp. 39-40).

Among the large single images that stand out at the other pole of the composition the giants impose themselves most distinctly in the first two books. In the rest of the work reference to their size is most often neglected and in many a scene they appear vaguely normal. [141]

At certain significant points of the tale the author interprets their size by associating them with tremendous amount of matter. Such are the chapters that show Gargantua and Pantagruel swallowing great quantities of food and drink or being clothed with wearing apparel of huge measurements (Garg., iii, iv, vii, viii; *Pant.*, iv).

Some of these incidents have excellent corporeality and plasticity. Remarkable in this respect is the narrative in which Pantagruel is seen getting up with a cradle chained on his back. The phenomenon looks to Rabelais like a five hundred ton vessel standing up on one end (*Pant.*, iv, p. 185). Let us mention here also Bringuenarilles who feeds on windmills with their sails open (IV, xvii, pp. 587-588).

Most often, however, immensity is brought into view by its contrast with things normal. The reader then moves along, as Spitzer so aptly put it, on the narrow strip that separates reality from unreality, [142] the regular from the enormous universe. In this strange game both the real and the fantastic move out of their own places and become dubious by their mutual contact. The comical effects thus attained are sinister. Everyday objects that associate with monstruous ones acquire unfamiliar characteristics and make us shudder. On the other hand, fabulous things loose their poetic flavor and frighten us in a realistic setting. This is the climate of the Picrocholine war. All the familiar sights of Rabelais's childhood residence, the *Chinonais*, retain some of their identity while turning into a battle-ground of giants (*Garg.*, xv-xliv, pp. 78-129).

The awesome chapter in which the author enters the mouth of Pantagruel and there finds French cities and villages, lead us in our analysis from the giants to the landscapes (*Pant.*, xxxii, pp. 305-308). The giants here actually acquire some aspects of a natural scene. The author marches along on Pantagruel's outstretched tongue as if on a road and his teeth look to him like mountains. He comes accross a peasant planting cabbage, a town as big as Rouen or Nantes, and

---

[141] Of course the first two books also contain such passages, e.g. the chapters dealing with Gargantua's education: *Garg.*, XIV, XV, XXI, XXII, XXIII, XXIV.

[142] Leo Spitzer, "Le prétendu réalisme de Rabelais," *Modern Philology*, XXXVII (November 1939), p. 142.

on top of one of the teeth he finds a *jeu de paume,* beautiful galeries, vineyards and many country houses. The picture has excellent contours and lively detail.

In contrast to the image of giants, space filled in with solid matter, the materiality of the landscapes is sparse and lofty. In a horizontal sense they contain extensive areas of land and sea. In their tri-dimensional aspects they rise high into the sky and to the astronomical universe. They will be studied at this point mostly in the *Quart Livre* because it is here they reach their climax.

On the horizontal plane it is of course the sea that plays an outstanding part in the fourth book, the theme being a maritime voyage over a large section of the globe, leading from the French west coast to the regions of Northern China, accross the Atlantic, the Pacific and the seas of the so called North-Western passage then believed to connect them. [143] Rabelais's infauation with sea travel and the discovery of land is easily associated with that of actual voyagers, the Portuguese, the Spaniards, the English and the French, a literary expression of the same Renaissance aspiration for the penetration of space. The very taste of the author for navigation reveals that drive: the detailed and affectionate description of ships at port, of their crews, of figures carved as symbols under the sterns, of operations at calm and in the storm would give us an idea of the wide open sea even if it were not described elsewhere (IV, i, pp. 538-540; xviii, pp. 593-594; lxiii, pp. 713-714).

The book as a whole conveys distance from the beginning by its refernce to the extensive geographical area to be covered. As the story unfolds this impression is enhanced by descriptions of the numerous islands the expedition encountered.

In the detail of the text distance materializes in the linear pattern that evolves from the depiction of the motion of vessels propelled by oars but particularly by the wind. Rabelais is spellbound by the moving power of the wind. At one point he evokes god Aeolus' leather bottle filled with that element and given to Ulysses so he could navigate when the wheather was calm (IV, xliii, p. 657). [144]

---

[143] Abel Lefranc, *Les navigations de Pantagruel* (Paris, 1904), pp. 49-50. We omitted the fifth book because of its doubtful authenticity.

[144] *Odyssey,* Ch. X, V. 19 et seq.

Rabelais likes to describe a boat with the wind in its back gliding rapidly over the surface of the water, because speed helps to conceive of range. The following sentence taken from the trip to Utopia is a fine example: "De faict, une heure après, se leva le vent nommé nord-nord-west auqel ilz donnèrent pleines voilles, et prindrent la haulte mer, et, en briefs jours, passans par Porto Sancto et par Madère, firent scalle ès isles de Canarre" (*Pant*, xxiv, p. 271). The considerable length of a horizontal line here is made tangible by the speed with which it is drawn from one end to another. The brevity of the sentence underlines the velocity of the motion, making the visual experience all the more vivid. In a picturesque passage of the fourth book distance is expressed through speed stylistically by metaphors and comparisons. Gargantua has sent a boat after his son which, thanks to its unusual celerity was able to catch up with him during his stay in the remote island of Medamothi (IV, iii, pp. 545-548). The vessel bore as a symbol attached to its stern a flying fish called *hirondelle de mer*. The notion of flight serves to express the rapidity of the vehicle and this is stressed by its name *Chelidoine*, a frenchified version of the Greek word for swallow. [145] The watercraft flies like a bird over the waves: "Ainsi estoit ce vaisseau légier comme une hirondelle, de sort que plustoust sembloit sus mer voler que voguer" (p. 546).

Excellent are the three-dimensional vistas of the fourth book and most striking among them is the description of the storm that encompasses the sky, the wind, the air and the sea (IV, xviii, p. 592). Remote points of nature here reach out for one another. The waves come up from the "depth of the sea," rise mountain high and are "suspended" there by the typhoon. At the same time gusts of wind and hail and lightning come down from above. The light effects make space tangible to the senses. Some of the lightning is white, some zigzag, says Rabelais combining color and motion for a contrast with the darkened air that has lost its translucency. At the end all the elements, all parts of the universe seem to mingle and form a chaotic whole.

While in all the above passages the wind is a mere force, a producer of visual realities and no visual reality in itself, in one fantastic

---

[145] χελιδών.

chapter of the fourth book it presents itself emphatically as matter, a large spatial phenomenon in its own right. Indeed, in its corporeality it acquires characteristics of a solid object. The inhabitants of the island Ruach are wind-eaters (IV, xliii, xliv, pp. 655-659). They propell the food received from above into their mouths by devices that serve to promote the formation of wind or else direct it. Most people use feather, paper or linen fans for a flatware. The rich have windmills at their disposal and swallow at their banquets delicious gusts of sirocco, gardino, zephyr, etc. The giant Bringuenarilles has a special diet. He visits the island in springtime as a tourist in order to feed on windmills. He finds them tasty and they promote his digestion. It evidently is their close contact with the wind that makes them a tidbit and a medication. It is as if the wind had turned into a regular solid in its last step towards materiality.

Attractive are some of the large maritime sights that have little or nothing to do with the wind. The story of the frozen words has a particular appeal (IV, lv-lvi, pp. 689-694). Pantagruel and his companions were navigating at the edge of the "Glacial Sea" where they heard a medley of voices floating in the air and seeming to come from nowhere. These voices turned out to be battle sounds that froze in the cold of the previous winter and were now turning into sounds again as they thawed in the warmer weather. Floating in the sea, the frozen sounds had the shape of sugarplums, a few of which the pilot picked up and threw on deck. Warmed in one's hands, they melted like snow and sounded forth once more. Soon the air was filled with barbarous noises, human voices in an unknown language, the neighing of horses and clashes of weapons and armour. The aural experience involved here also has great visual appeal. The evocation of the atmosphere by the spreading of sound over the wide open sea builds to a landscape of considerable volume. And the tableau moves further up towards the sky with the mention of Nephelobates, or cloudwalkers, [146] the name of one of the nations supposed to have participated in the battle. The fighting must have taken place between the sea level and the clouds.

There are pure aerial views in the fourth book, spectacles that take us above the level of the sea. Like most Renaissance authors or

---

[146] A term created by Rabelais from the Greek words νεφέλη, cloud, and βατήρ, walker.

artists Rabelais is fascinated by the notion of flight that helps us to penetrate the elusive extension of atmospheric space. At one point he describes the speed of carrier pigeons, capable of covering in two hours a distance which a rapid sailboat with two or three rows of oars and with the wind behind it would travel in three days and three nights (IV, iii, p. 546). The bird "chops" the air, the author says, expressing here too his feeling for the materiality of the air. Not quite as sweeping but rather spectacular, fanciful and splendid as an expression of aerial corporeality, is the portrait of a flying pig, the god of the chitterlings, who appears in the sky above the island *Farouche* (IV, xli, p. 652). He is an awesome aerial phenomenon whose body shines with the colors of various precious stones.

Above the air, the firmament is evoked in one chapter of the fourth book. In contrast with the aerial regions, a subtle medium of unspecified height, it has solid characteristics. A superstitious fear that the sky may fall down on them is supposed to have beset certain nations and even certain species of birds (IV, xvii, pp. 588-589). The larks, we learn, are suffering from this phobia, as did a certain tribe of Celts who lived next to the Rhine and told of their anxiety to Alexander the Great. This sort of delusion, the discussion further states, was widespread in antiquity in spite of people's confidence that the columns held by Atlas were keeping heaven and earth asunder. Although the sky viewed as a ceiling tends to limit space the universe here does not seem diminished in size. It assumes a massive kind of grandeur.

There is also in the fourth book a reference to heaven, the spiritual version of the sky, an interesting intermezzo, because it embraces the physical and metaphysical universe as well. Over the solid basis of the earth hovers in indefinite colors the world above. There is a close pictorial relation between the two because the author here speaks of objects sent down by the Divinity to men. The theme evolves from a reference to the decretal that is hanging down from the ceiling of the temple of the *Papimanes*. It was written and sent down by a cherub to this nation. Disregarding the difference between the Christian heaven and Olympus, Rabelais, in this connection, mentions the tablets of law sent by God to Moses, the inscriptions dispatched by Appollo to the temple of Adelphi, the semblance of Cybele transmitted to Phrygia, and that of Diana to Tauris. He adds the *oriflamme* which God offered as a symbol to the French kings, the sharp edged buckler that came down from the sky to Rome under the reign of Numa Pompilius, and the statue of Minerva that descended to the Acropolis of Athens.

For a complete treatment of the theme of variety and grandeur, these two outstanding ingredients of Rabelaisian imagery might be considered in their organic relationship, within single pictorial units of the work. Variety sometimes decorates a tableau drawn in big outlines or even covers it in full; it can build up to it or merely appear on its margin. In some cases variety precedes and predicts large single images, in others it evolves from it, tapering off the scenery as a whole. Some of these relations will be found in the following analyses of a giant, a geographic sketch, a seascape and a cosmic narrative.

A description of Gargantua follows the pattern that leads from variety to grandeur. (*Garg.*, viii, pp. 26-30). In his effort to delineate the giant the author resorts at first to multitudinousness. He describes every bit of his attire, his shirt, his gusset, the doublet, the breeches, stockings, the flip-flap, the shoes, the jacket, belt, sword, purse, bonnet, plume and the jewelry. The mere enumeration of the items that cover the body of the colossus may give us an impression of its proportions by a subconscious awareness of the relation between number and size. But the large measurements of the wearing apparel add up more concretely to the phenomenon as a whole: "Pour sa chemise furent levées neuf cens aulnes de toilles... Pour son pourpoinct furent levées huyt cens treize aulnes de satin blanc, et pour les aguieillettes quinze cens neuf peaulx et demye de chiens... Pour ses chausses feurent levéz unze cens cinq aulnes et ung tiers d'estamet blanc..." etc. (pp. 26-27).

In geographic descriptions variety sometimes appears sporadically on the map and sometimes it builds up to territorial grandeur. Small geographic items, if lined up, lead to large sections of land. The motive makes its appearance on a small scale in the early part of Gargantua (*Garg.*, IV, p. 15). In the Picrocholine war it materializes twice, reaching in the one case fairly large, in the other tremendous proportions. In the first mentioned of these scenes, thirty cities located around the Loire and its tributaries are enumerated one by one for having promised their help to Grandgousier (*Garg.*, xlvii, pp. 135-136). But the theme reaches its climax in the military plan suggested

by the *fouaciers* to Picrochole (*Garg.*, xxxiii, pp. 97-102). The map
of a large section of the world then known unfolds little by little.
While describing the progression of the army, masses of cities, provinces, counties, duchies, countries, islands, rivers, seas and oceans
appear before our eyes, sometimes in a straight line, sometimes following an irregular pattern dictated undoubtedly by strategical con-
siderations. The author mentions more than 100 place names, and the
imaginary campaign involves most of Europe, part of Asia and Africa
and reaches up to Greenland and the Arctic Ocean. Although Rabelais
here mocks paper strategists carried away by their imagination, he
himself is passionately interested in the scheme and gets dizzy with
geography.

Among the many ways by which variety relates to grandeur in the
seascapes or landscapes, provocative is the relationship, implicit in
the description of the storm (IV, xviii, pp. 591-592). Variety here
introduces space. It plays an ominous part as a first restless manifestation of the spatial catastrophe to come. The wind announces its
coming by the motion of the sails on the boat. Rabelais enjoys their
diversity and exhibits his knowledge of their use and destination. The
storm we have analyzed elsewhere is signaled by the fluttering of
the ensign on the poop. At a general alert given to the crew the sails
are now lowered. They are itemized with great care and mostly by
their provençal names used in the Mediterranean: the foresail called
méjane, the *contreméjane,* the square-shaped *triou* used mostly when
fleeing the winds, the big sail called *maistrelle,* the *épagon* set on the
mizzenmast, the *civadière* placed below the bowsprit, the *boulingues*
or fore-sails, the main topsail, the small topsail and all the yards go
down so that at the end only the ratline and the shroud are standing.

In the cosmic image that evolves from Panurge's praise of the
relationship between creditors and debtors variety and spatial effects
are intertwined and inseparable from each other (III, iii, iv, pp. 338-
346). In this declamation Panurge answers Pantagruel, who admon-
ished him because as a castellan of Salmagundi he squandered his
income and ran into debt. Carried away by his own eloquence, Panurge comes to the conclusion that the harmony of the whole plane-
tary system, of the elements, and of the human body is based on the
principle of borrowing and lending. The passage presents a Rabelaisian macrocosm and microcosm, and in some ways predicts Pascal's

"Disproportion de l'homme." [147] The universe Rabelais depicts depends for its size on antique imagery, on the theory of the spheres, and on that of the multiplicity of the worlds as propounded by Metrodorus and by Petron of Himera. Taking advantage of the Olympic names of the planets, he also conjures mythological sites of cosmic proportions. Inspired by a beautiful scene in the *Iliad* [148] he shows all things existent dangling over space on a golden chain set up by Jupiter on Olympus: "Jupiter... avecques sa chaîne homéricque suspendera toutes les intelligences, dieux, cieulx, daemons, génies, héroes, diables, terre, mer, tous élémens" (III, iii, p. 341). Effects of light and darkness between the sun and the stars make the image particularly spectacular. His eyes moving gradually downward, the author then evokes the theory according to which the earth exhales vapors to the stars for their alimentation. The airy space between the globe and the planets thereby become tangible. In a discussion of the transmutation of the elements, the description stops for a moment on the surface of the earth, then loses itself in the depth of the human body.

The variety of the tableau is as dazzling as its size. While proceeding from large to small, Rabelais enumerates planets, gods, elements, titans and giants, the spirits of antiquity and Christianity, and parts and organs of the human body.

We have left to the end passages where both the drive for diversity and for spatial expansion mingle with an aspiration to beauty. [149] Characteristically, in these chapters the ideal of antiquity acquires great importance. Greek words or individuals with Greek names — found, of course, elsewhere in Rabelais — here move into the foreground and dominate the scene as a source of inspiration to the tone and the mood of the description.

Outstanding among these themes is Gargantua's education under Ponocrates and the *Abbaye de Theleme*. Although related to each other, the artistic principles of the passages differ in that the first

---

[147] In our conclusion we shall discuss such aspects of Pascal's universe that set it apart from anything written in the sixteenth century.

[148] Bk. VIII, I, 19 et seq.; also Bk. XV, I, 19.

[149] Rabelais's ability to create beauty has not always been recognized by his critics: v. Emile Gebhardt, *Rabelais* (Paris, s.d.), p. 71: "L'esprit de Rabelais n'est pas porté vers la beauté," and "La grande poésie des choses visibles ne s'est point levé en son esprit."

one shows harmony in motion, the second shows it at rest. They remind this critic of a similar twin creation in Greek art, the sculptured groups on the two gables of the temple in Olympia. [150] The one located on the west side represents the war between Lapiths and Centaurs and is marked by action. That of the east side shows figures in a state of repose before a chariot race. The individual grace of the works and the contrast in their rhythm is an experience highly satisfying to the eye. Beauty linked with antiquity is essential to Rabelais's concept of the ideal education and develops in contrast to the ungainly habits Gargantua acquired in the scholastic atmosphere of his early upbringing (*Garg.*, xxi, pp. 62-64). An introductory passage illustrates the change. Young Eudémon, the first of the instructors to appear in the tale, is so well groomed he looks like a little angel. He makes a speech "Proféré avecques gestes tant propres, pronunciation tant distincte, voix tant éloquente et languaige tant aorné et bien latin, que mieulx resembloit un Gracchus, un Cicéron ou un Emilius du temps passé qu'un juvenceau de se siècle" (*Garg.*, xv, p. 50).

The Greek atmosphere is established with all its esthetic values at the beginning of the main chapter on education (*Garg.*, xxiii, pp. 68-75). In order to cleanse the pupil's mind, a doctor by the Greek name of Theodore has him take Hellebore, a herb used against insanity in antiquity. Moreover, all of Gargantua's masters, Ponocrates, Anagnostes, Gymnaste and Eudémon have Greek names. [151]

Images of physical beauty here mingle with precepts of hygiene. As soon as he gets up, Gargantua is rubbed down, then dressed, combed, curled, ornamented and perfumed. After the morning sports, he is rubbed down once more and changes his shirt. At the end of his midday meal, he washes his hands and his eyes "de belle eau fraische" (p. 71). The frequent allusion to attractive corporeal habits are insinuating and spread their character to the description of sports.

Without being defined precisely, the particular traits of beauty are revealed by the rhythm peculiar to the acts of the individuals:

---

[150] For the identity of the sculptors and the unity of the composition as a whole, v. Buschos and Hamann, *Die Skulpturen des Zeustempels zu Olympia* (Marburg, 1924).

[151] The teachers may be considered humanists with Greek pseudonyms or they may be veritable Greeks transplanted from antiquity into the complex milieu of the tale, a melting pot of heterogeneous elements.

a free, unconstrained, and almost leisurely bearing, reminiscent of bodily attitudes found in works of art of antiquity. It is apparent in intellectual as well as physical proceedings and has earlier impressed itself in the facility and grace of Eudémon's speech rendered verbatim by Rabelais (*Garg.*, xv, p. 50). It is analytically exposed in the principle chapter on education. When after their morning studies teacher and pupil apply theoretical wisdom to the human condition, the exercise is not limited in time: sometimes it lasts for hours and sometimes it is over in a few minutes (*Garg.*, xxiii, p. 69). With a similar informality Gargantua engages in ball games: "Tout leur jeu n'estoit qu'en liberté, car ilz laissoient la partie quant leur plaisoit et cessoient ordinairement lorsque suoient parmy le corps, ou estoient aultrement las" (*Garg.*, xxiii, p. 70). And unconstraint reaches its climax in the spontaneous study of biology through dishes served during the midday meal and in the study of arithmetic through card games played in the afternoon and evening. Such fundamental principles of conduct must necessarily be evident in the motions of the individuals and thereby they partake of the author's artistic intentions.

While in the absence of spatial effects Rabelais here gives full vent to his passion for variety, the exuberance of the total tableau does not interfere with the good balance of individual images. Everyone of Gargantua's numerous performances is executed with freedom, beauty and ease, whether he plays ball or swims or rows or fences or rides on horseback or jousts or hunts or shoots at targets or throws the javelin or runs up a mountain or jumps over ditches or climbs on trees or plays musical instruments or watches the stars or prays.

In the case of the *Abbaye de Thélème* Greek antiquity imposes itself in the very name of the institution and in that of its six towers (*Garg.*, liii, pp. 149-151). The smile of Attica seems to spread all over the structure.

We are back to the two main components of Rabelaisian imagery, to variety and spatial grandeur. They turn into an artistic design inspired by contemporary architecture. [152] Large spaces present themselves with harmony and serenity, and within this framework variety

---

[152] With regard to style and presentation the passage may be inspired by Aristotle's discussions on education. (*Politics*, VIII, 1337 b, 1338 a and b, 1339 b, 1340 b.)

is found in the richness of the ornament. The two great visual principles of the author here are poured into a static image and stand still.

Spatial representations derive their esthetic effects from architectural geometry. [153] As the building unfolds, ample planes and volumes
follow each other in a vertical or horizontal sense with well-balanced
regularity. The author's eyes move from floor to floor, from the top
floor to the roof, and then down the basement. Simultaneously vast
libraries, staircases, galleries, halls and apartments come into sight.
The voluminousness and equilibrium of single portions of the building
is defined sometimes with particular care. Splendid is the account of
the spiral staircase: "Au mylieu estoit une merveilleuse viz, de laquelle
l'entrée estoit par le dehors du logis en un arceau large de six toizes.
Icelle estoit faicte de telle symmétrie et capacité que six hommes
d'armes, la lance sus la cuisse, povoient de front ensemble monter
jusques au dessus de tout le bastiment" (p. 151). With the description
of parks, gardens, and areas of sports and entertainment found in the
inner court and around the chateau, artistic geometry and grandeur
move into the outdoors (*Garg.*, lv, pp. 154-156). And the airiness of
the building seems to blend with nature. The names of the towers
take us by association into every direction of the compass and into
the atmosphere of the earth (*Garg.*, liii, p. 150). The names *Artice,
Anatole, Mesembrine,* and *Hesperie* come from the Greek words for
north, east, south and west. A fifth tower situated in the northwest
and called *Cryere* — the icy one — derives its name evidently from
the fact that it is exposed to the cold *galerne,* the wind that comes
from the Atlantic. The notion of the wind passing over the ocean
adds an element of breeziness to the spatial effect. In contrast to it,
on the opposite side, in the southeast corner stands the tower *Calaer*
or beatiful air, a symbol of sunshine and atmospheric warmth that
completes the panorama. Beyond its physical limits the abbey spreads
out into the cosmos.

Variety is apparent in the luxuriance of the architectural detail,
in the decoration of the walls, the ceilings, the roof, in the many
colored marbles used for staircase, in the furniture, tapestry and

---

[153] Jean Plattard, *La vie et l'œuvre de Rabelais* (Paris, 1939), pp. 55-56.
Paul Vitry, *Hôtels et maisons de la Renaissance française* (Paris, 1910), II,
ii et seq.

carpets, in the jets spouting from the fountain, and the multitude of animals painted in the inner gallery.

As far as imaginative force is concerned, there probably is nothing comparable to the visual drama of Rabelais. It looks like a powerful monument of the past towards the next century, the period of classicism, in whose literary works the exterior world will pale, giving place to the observation of the inner workings of man and the universe.

CHAPTER **IV**

RONSARD

In their aesthetic aspect variety and magnitude reach their highlight in sixteenth century French literature in Pierre de Ronsard. Essential differences between his amplitude and that of Rabelais, whom we have just discussed, depend, of course, on the genre. They are a matter of pace, of gesture, of formation. In Rabelais, the humorist, the multitude of images follow one another with abrupt motions: their relationship is angular, their edges are uneven. They are marked by automatism, to use the oft repeated expression Bergson has created to describe humor. No such word is known for a definition of lyricism. In Ronsard the accumulated elements of the design move along gently. Their outlines are soft, they touch at each other with ease, they seem to embrace one another. In both cases the broad milieu presented is soothing to the eye. And multitude and space together give us a feel of the infinite. The former by the restless and ever moving impulse behind it, the latter by emotions aroused through the contemplation of distance.

Ronsard's sceneries may be divided into landscapes and cosmic vistas. The former reproduce the experience of the eye, the latter are visual abstractions. The difference actually depends on the point of observation taken by the author. In the landscapes he stands on the surface of the earth, in the cosmic images he takes his position outside of the universe, in empty space as it were. His change of the perspective leads to separate genres that must be treated apart.

To make the Renaissance characteristics of Ronsard's landscapes stand out, we will introduce our analysis with a short commentary of a well known fifteenth century poem, a description of nature by

Charles d'Orléans. It is typical of its time and creates diversity in a cozy milieu:

> Le temps a laissé son manteau
> De vent, de froidure et de pluye
> Et s'est vestu de brouderie,
> De soleil luyant, cher et beau.
>   Il n'y a beste, ne oyseau,
> Qu'en son jargon ne chante ou crie:
> Le temps a laissé son manteau.
>   Rivière, fontaine et ruisseau
> Portent en livree jolie,
> Gouttes d'argent d'orfeverie,
> Chascun s'habille de nouveau:
> Le temps a laissé son manteau. [154]

We have here a landscape rich in detail and limited in scope. Although rather airy, its charm depends on its intimacy and its blurred visual effects. The consecutive metaphors that associate natural phenomena with articles of clothing give a gentle sort of domesticity to the cosmos and provide it with the vaguely defined yet quite confining outline of a human individual. Restrained by its feudal garb, the sunlight receives sligtly static characteristics, and so do the wind and the rain, otherwise excellent means for the creation of spatial volume.

Nothing stands in the way of the free and clear development of space in the sceneries of Ronsard. In his description horizontal planes multiply and mountains rise towards the sky. The atmosphere that hovers above the earth is boundless. In an effort to fathom its depth, the author depicts the flight of birds and mythological figures. The breezy tableaux thus created are full of pictorial detail. The earth bursts forth in fertility and abundance, its shapes and colors mingling with those of the sky and the rainbow. And all these phenomena depend on space and move into space.

The sun is in Ronsard the natural source and descriptive medium of both space and variety. An image of their growth will be shown in the following passages taken from various spots of the work of

---

[154] Charles d'Orléans, *Poésies,* ed. Pierre Champion (Paris, 1927), II, 307-308. "Les fourriers d'esté sont venus" (II, 307) is similar in style but not as rich in metaphors and natural images.

Ronsard. The order of the selections is of our own making and serves
to highlight a valid point. For Ronsard's amplitude can best be ap-
praised by a presentation of its gradual increase. In our quotations the
sun will be seen at first at dusk then at noon and finally during
the whole day, whereby spaces will evolve to their full cosmic size.
Then the response of the earth's fertility will be observed under the
touch of the sun: at first a single flower will open below the firmament,
then masses of many-colored flowers will appear, and finally a full
landscape with rich vegetation. In the process we will refer briefly
here and there to Ronsard's source material, in order to sense his rich
poetical heritage and indicate further aspects of his originality.

Descriptions of the early morning are serene and have great charm:

> Mais aussi tost que l'aube aux doigts rosins
> Eschevelée eut tous les lieus voisins
> Ensaffrané, & que la tresse blonde
> Du grand Soleil s'esparpilla sur l'onde [155]

Here, as in some of the subsequent passages, the sun rises from the
ocean, a poetic vision borrowed from Greek antiquity [156] which, atyp-
ical as it may be of French lyricism, perfectly fits Ronsard's artistic
schema. Nature lovers from Chateaubriand to some present literary
critics have objected to the mingling of antique images with natural
descriptions. Whereas it is an alleged lack of descriptive purity that
irked the Romantics, later commentators lament the author's snubbing
of the rules of realism. [157] Yet the Renaissance, which removed the
limits of time (as well as of space) and was unwilling to remain
within the confines of contemporary life, had the gift to form from
the past and the present a splendid, supratemporal whole. Without
comprehending fully the metaphysical aspects of the Greek universe,
Ronsard combines it harmoniously with French sceneries. Thus the
Attic sunrise that in the above poem happens to blend with the image
of Saint-Germain-en-Laye is artistically well conceived and raises the

---

[155] Ronsard, *Œuvres complètes,* ed. Paul Laumonier (Paris, 1914-1967),
II, p. 148.

[156] e.g. *Odyssey,* beginnings of II, III, V, XVII.

[157] Chateaubriand, *Œuvres complètes* (Paris: Pourrat Frères, 1836), XV,
107-108. Dudley B. Wilson, *Ronsard Poet of Nature* (Manchester, 1961),
pp. 23, 56.

theme to a timeless level. [158] It also expresses the author's particular intentions, for the simultaneous presentation of the sky with the ocean offers tremendous volume. The intimation rather than the full development of space in the early morning is very effective and leaves us awe-struck with latent grandeur. The rosy emanation of the sun towards the sky and its spreading of a whitish tint over the waves serve to underline the widening of horizons in both directions.

More can be seen in a scene taken from the *Franciade*. The sun now appears to have left the waters. It throws its light over the sky and a touch of saffron replaces at this point the colors of the daybreak:

> Quand le Soleil perruqué de lumiere
> Eut de Thetis sa vieille nourrisiere
> En se levant abandonné les eaux,
> Et fait grimper contre-mont ses chevaux,
> Et que l'Aurore à la main saffranée
> Eut annoncé la clarté retournée
>
> (XVI, p. 250)

The mythological symbolism here applied, contrary to the metaphorical imagery of the poem of Charles d'Orléans discussed above, expresses motion, and far from limiting space, helps to display it. The representation of Apollo arising from the sea and of his horsedrawn chariot climbing up the sky are effective in this respect. Nor do Aurora's fingers, possibly upheld, interfere with the dynamics of the scene, because fingers are light and movable. Only the association of the sun's rays with a headdress may have a slightly obstructing effect.

In a poem dedicated to Jehan de Thiers, Ronsard follows the course of the sun during the entire day:

> Car soit que le soleil abandonne la source
> De son hoste Ocean, & apreste à la course
> Son char, à qui l'Aurore a de sa belle main
> Attelé les chevaux & rangez sous le frein:
> Ou soit qu'en plein midi ses rayons il nous darde,
> Et à plomb dessous luy toutes choses regarde:

---

[158] Of course a sunrise observed purely from nature can have great charm: Petrarca, *Rime* (Livorno, 1876), p. 210: "Il cantar novo, e 'l pianger de gli augelli."

Ou soit qu'en devallant plein de soif et d'ahan,
Il s'aille rebaigner es flots de l'Ocean,
Et que son char en garde aux Dieux marins il baille:
Ton esprit n'a repos

(X, pp. 40-41)

It is the firmament that stands out most clearly in this description.
The poet only touches the ocean in the morning and at nightfall with
light and offers no more than a general and unspecified impression
of "all things" in the noon light. Very Greek is the mythological
notion of the sun's immersion in the sea, its arising from the depth
of the waters in the morning and its bathing in them at night, a
hydromechanical illusion of appaling proportions.

In the rising Ronsardian symphony as we present it, we shall see
at this point the first traces of the life giving forces of the sun, a
herald, as it were, of variety and fertility to come. A single marigold
will be seen opening and closing its petals as the sun appears in the
morning and disappears at night:

Quand le Soleil, ton amoureux, s'abaisse
Dedans le sein de Thetis son hostesse,
Allant revoir le Pere de la Mer,
On voit ton chef se clorre & se fermer,
Palle, deffait: mais quand sa tresse blonde
A grands bouquetz s'eparpille sur l'onde
Se reveillant, tu t'esveilles joyeux,
Et pour le voir tu dessilles tes yeux,
Et sa clarté est seule ton envie,
Un seul Soleil te donnant mort et vie.

(XV, p. 175)

In writing these lovely lines on the *souci* Ronsard may have re-
membered two verses by Petrarca [159] who deals with the theme swiftly
and parenthetically. In a general way Petrarca's natural sceneries are
more rapid, more elegant and also more delicate. Ronsard can be
absorbed by detail. His descriptions are more copious, more over-
grown, more organic.

This is evidenced by our next passage, a further item in our
interpretation of fertility. It may have come to the author while

---

[159] *Ibid.*, p. 246: "Che quando nasce, e mor' fior, e foglia."

reading Marullo and deals with the violet that emerges with a great
variety or colors from under the sun.[160] This remarkable floral spec-
imen branches out into no less that 250 species, each having its
distinct shape and hew. Within this caleidoscopic whole, certain kinds
have several shapes and colors of their own. Following a widespread
trend in Renaissance poetry, Ronsard compares in these lines nature
to his beloved:

> Or tout ainsi que cette fleur ne porte
> Teint ny beauté d'une semblable sorte,
> Vostre beauté diverse tout aussi,
> Elle est vermeille & vous estes vermeille,
> Sa blancheur est à la vostre pareille,
> L'une est d'azur, vostre esprit et vos yeux
> Ont pour leur but le bel azur des cieux.
>   L'une a le gris pour sa pareure mise
> Et vous aymez la belle couleur grise.
> L'une bigarre & colore son teint
> De cent beautez de qui le vostre est peint
>
>   (XIV, pp. 149-150)

Numerous flowers put together will reach a similar effect. In an
ode inspired by Horace and written in praise of wine, Ronsard extolls
the flower of the vine that he professes to prefer to the most beautiful
flowers on earth (X, pp. 129-132). In the process he evokes roses,
red carnations, two kinds of hyacinths, marigolds, daffodils, the
violette de mars, the elecampane, the arum and the lily. Four shades
of red, three shades of yellow, two shades of white and green are
mentioned or implied as the description unfolds. Particularly fine is
the distinction between the reds, the light red of the rose, the darker
one of the carnation, the reddish and purplish tint of one of the
hyacinths, the bright yellowish red of the other. It should be noted
that the flowers are not mentioned by name but are referred to by a
poetic interpretation of their origins as handed down by mythological
lore. The learned would see through the riddle and enjoy the marginal
introduction of antiquity. From an artistic point of view the quick
moving scenes here presented add graphic variety to the motley of
colors. Adonis wounded in his thigh, the youth Hyacinthus killed by

---

[160] *Carmina* (Turici, 1951), p. 10: "Has violas atque haec tibi candida
lilia mitto."

Apollo's arrow, Ajax committing suicide, Narcissus falling into the river, Helen bathed in tears, Juno breastfeeding Mars: these are the episodes that flash by as the images of flowers appear one by one.

When variety relates to space, Ronsard's art appears in full. Following is a wide open and copious landscape with representations of the sky, the air, the land and sea and mountains and forests and flowers and animal life:

> Et loin du populace allons oüir la vois
> De dix mile oiselets qui se plaignent es bois.
> Ja des monts contreval les tiedes neiges chéent,
> Ja les ouvertes fleurs par les campagnes béent,
> Ja l'épineus rosier deplie ses boutons
> Au lever du soleil, qui semblent aus tetons
> Des filles de quinze ans, quand le sein leur pommelle,
> Des filles de quinze ans, quand
> Et s'esleve bossé d'une enfleure jumelle.
> Ja la mer gist couchée en son grand lit espars
> Ja Zephire murmure
>
> (VI, p. 73)

Of great interest is the compositional pattern of Ronsard's landscapes. It has been observed that the multitude of his images evolve around a central factor in these tableaux. [161] Yet it seems that sort of composition is rare and altogether contrary to the principles of his art. His eyes are constantly on the move and as the phenomena multiply they gather around a progressing line or a progressing plane that wanders about feeely and reaches its balance in space. Such lines or planes move essentially either in a horizontal or a vertical direction although they spread at times from the main to the secondary area. Thus the horizontal sights rise slightly or even quite considerably into the air, while those that traverse the upper regions often spread out on the ground. In some cases we have composite images that go from the horizontal to the vertical and vice-versa. And variety materializes along the main line of composition.

The above-mentioned vista is of the horizontal kind. Its components, particularly the forest, the mountains and the sea, add up to a broad surface. The presence of the sun, the birds and the wind

---

[161] Dudley B. Wilson, *Ronsard Poet of Nature*, pp. 20-24.

gently lift the scene from its main position on the ground into higher regions. Fertility and variety move along the horizontal. The green of the forest, the white of the snow-covered mountains, the red of the roses and the blue of the sea make for a picturesque ensemble. The comparison of the rosebush to the growing teats of the breast of a young woman deepens the sense of fertility imparted by the concrete figures of the scenery.

Sometimes the author creates horizontal parallels, one in the air, the other on the earth, as is the case in the following beautiful tableau, the upper part of which evolves from the flight of birds whereas the lower one shows masses of birds dwelling on the ground:

> Ainsi qu'on voit les bien-volantes grues
> Crier aigu, quand passer il leur faut
> La mer pour vivre en un païs plus chaud.
> Autant qu'on voit d'oiseaus de tous plumages,
> Au mois d'avril, hostes des marescages,
> S'amonceler pour pondre et pour couver
> L'un à fleur d'eau ses plumes vient laver,
> L'autre sous l'eau tient ses ailes plongées,
> Et l'autre pesche à friandes gorgées,
> Et l'autre tourne à l'entour de son ny,
> Peuple emplumé, innombrable, infini,
> Qui en volant sur les rives cognües
> Se presse ensemble aussi espais que nües. [162]

In contrast to the upper plane formed by motion, the lower one is static and multiform, an eldorado of avial life in a marchland. Proliferation is illustrated by its principle, the laying of eggs and their hatching, and it is actually manifest to the eye by the multitude of the birds. Great is the variety apparent in their positions and actions. Some are on the water, some underneath, some are in the act of plunging. Again others are on land and in the air. Entertaining is the diversity of their motions, their washing, their fishing, their turning around their nests, their flying in thick masses over the shores. The image is brilliant and lifelike. It is inspired by several passages of

---

[162] Ronsard, *Œuvres complètes* (Paris: Bibliothèque de la Pléiade, 1950), I, 667. Because of the special appeal of some of its imagery we are using occasionally the text of 1584.

the *Iliad* and the *Aeneid* [163] but the contrast between motion and rest
and the detailed observation of bird life in the marches belong to
Ronsard. He is more picturesque than his antique models. [164] Pleasure
taken in eminently colorful representations of life reverts to the Middle
Ages and may be inherent in Christian civilization.

The vertically oriented compositions sometimes point upward,
sometimes downward, in certain cases consecutively in both directions.
Such scenes can be narrow in appearance, moving closely around their
axis, or they can be bulky, involving large sections of the sky and
the air. Often they are traced by the flight of birds or other flying
objects, the most concrete means of depicting aerial space.

The famous ode of the hawthorn: "Bel aubepin fleurissant" (VI,
pp. 242-244) materializes first along an ascending then a descending
line. Too well known to be quoted, we shall merely analyze its composition. The mentioning of a river at the outstart of the poem serves
to extend the scene slightly in the horizontal. Then we move up from
its roots through the trunk to the top of the shrub where the night-
ingale has built its nest. The presence of the birds raises the figure
by association with flight into airy space. The symphony ends with
a downward motion from way above. While expressing his wish that
the hawthorn will never be hurled don by lightning, the wind, the axe
or by time, the poet evokes in spite of the negative statement, the
image of the trunk tumbling to the ground under the impact of
the elements. Expressions of fertility move at first from the outside
to the inside of the hawthorn, then follow the line of composition bottom to top. Its exterior is verdent and bloomming. Hawthorns can have
red, pink or white flowers and perhaps Ronsard had all of them in
mind. The wild wine further contributes to the luxuriance of the
image. Inside the object is bursting with insect life. Red ants are
swarming in its bottom and bees have settled in its trunk. The moss
and the silk in the nest add a gentle element of wealth to the description.

Ronsard addressed two poems to the lark and they have some
similarity of detail. Their imagery is light like the air and recalls

---

[163] *Iliad* II, 459-463 and III beginning; *Aeneid* VII, 698 et seq. and X,
264 et seq.
[164] Laumonier, *Ronsard poète lyrique* (Paris, 1932), p. 444.

vaguely Bernard de Ventadour's "Quan vey la laudeta mover" [165] except for the detailed observation of flight they contain. One of them shows the bird flying up then dropping down to the ground. The other finds it in the air then has it swoop down and finally fly up again. In either case variety materializes between the flights while the bird is on the thé ground. Because of their resemblence we shall omit quoting the first one mentioned, which is less well known although it has a great deal of charm. It shows the bird shaking the dew off its body in the air, performing little motions with its wings and ascending gradually with small leaps towards the sky. After having suddenly dropped, it is seen feeding and taking nourishment to its small. A lively image of insect life thereby appears on the ground (VII, p. 289). A short passages taken from the "Ode à l'Aloüette" will illustrate the character of these poems:

> Si tost que tu es arrosée
> Au point du jour, de la rosée,
> Tu fais en l'air mille discours:
> En l'air des ailes tu fretilles
> Et pendue au ciel, tu babilles,
> Et contes aus vens tes amours.
>
> Puis du ciel tu te laisses fondre,
> Dans un sillon vert, soit pour pondre,
> Soit pour esclorre, ou pour couver,
> Soit pour aporter la beschée
> A tes petits, ou d'une achée
> Ou d'une chenille, ou d'un ver.
>
> (VI, p. 246)

The birds "hanging" in air, an avial feat several times mentioned by Ronsard, and the short and lively motions of its wings as implied in the verb "frétiller" are well suited to make air in its immensity palpable to our sense of touch. With the airiness of the first stanza contrasts the impression of earthly abundance given in the second, the comfortable image of procreation and nurture on the ground.

Downward compositions sometimes are complex. At one point in the *Franciade* Ronsard combines the flight of the god Mercury with

---

[165] Raynouard, *Choix de poésies des troubadours*, III, 68.

that of the eagle. The two performances are compared and conceived of as a unit. The "double object" approaches the ground from unknown heights with great speed. It circles above a fairly large piece of earth and finally lands at a given point (XVI, p. 656).

In the supra-terranean compositions we have so far analyzed images that were in motion. Sometimes the dynamic effect of the representation is not caused by the rise or fall of the object but by the motion of the eye of the observer who describes altogether quiescent figures placed underneath or above each other in space. In such cases the description is not disposed closely around a line or an axis but carries along large sections of the cosmos. To this group belongs a lovely spring song, the ode: "Dieu vous gard, messagers fidelles" (VII, p. 294). Its tone having elements of trouvère poetry and its imagery being divided meticoulessly into three it has some medieval characteristics. Yet its spatial concept and variety are of the Renaissance. The spectacle takes us down to earth and then slightly up into the air again in a succession of images that show birds fluttering in the air followed by flowers on the ground and finally by butterflies and bees flying around above them.

We left to the end the sonnet that may be considered one of Ronsard's masterpieces:

> Ciel, Air, & vents, plains & montz descouvers,
>   Tertres fourchuz, & forestz verdoyantes
>   Rivages tortz, & sources ondoyantes,
>   Taillis razez, & vous bocages verds,
>
> Antres moussus à demyfront ouvers,
>   Prez, boutons, fleurs, & herbes rousoyantes,
>   Coustaux vineux, et plages blondoyantes
>   Gastine, Loyr, & vous mes tristes vers:
>
> Puis qu'au partir, rongé de soing & d'ire,
>   A ce bel œil, l'Adieu je n'ay sceu dire,
>   Qui pres & loing me detient en esmoy:
>
> Je vous supply, Ciel, air, ventz, montz, & plaines,
>   Tailliz, forestz, rivages & fontaines,
>   Antres, prez, fleurs, dictes le luy pour moy.
>
> (IV, 59-60)

The poet here gives an all encompassing impression of the universe with no spatial interruptions, with a feeling of great aerial expanse above and abundance on earth below. [166] While descending from the sky to the ground and then spreading out horizontally, the composition moves without any perfect regularity and yet in a definite pattern from big to small towards a central point and then back to the big again. Here is the detail of this splendid design: after evokation of the sky, the air, the winds, there come into view on an ever descreasing scale the still wide area of a plain, then a mountain, then hillocks, forests, rivers and springs and finally green groves and moss-covered dens. We are nearing the center of the composition, evidently the spot where the author is standing. Next to us, as it were, we can see a field, in the field a flower, then a bud and finally a dew drop on a blade of grass. At the end of the description the author's eyes stray once more away into the distance. With the image of slopes, light colored beaches and rivers he returns to nature at large. The diminution and increase of the figures give us an impression of earthly totality and permit us at the same time to focus our eyes on every object, big or small, because of its unique position within the whole of the artstic plan. The reiteration in the last two stanzas of most of the phenomena mentioned, with the suggestion that they echo the author's message to his beloved, seems to spread the visual adventure through the multiplication of sound into regions unknown — perhaps the infinite.

We are coming to the cosmic vistas of Ronsard, most of them hymns or odes and in all cases lengthy compositions. They revert mostly to Roman or Greek antiquity, to the Italian Renaissance and in some cases to the Middle Ages. Thematically speaking they arise from mythology, astronomy, the Old Testament, philosophy, theology and folklore.

From each of these domains they receive a pictorial quality of splendor that the author turns into his own. Those inspired by antiquity, as is the "Ode à Michel de l'Hospital" [167] are seen from a point in space that is near enough to observe small detail; they take

---

[166] Astemio Bevilacqua's "Herbe felici e prato aventuroso" that served as a model to this poem, offers a gentle, flowery, two-dimensional image. (*Rime di diversi*, 1547, 1053 V°; Joseph Vianey, *Le Pétrarquisme en France au XVIe siècle* (Montpellier, 1909), pp. 152-153.

[167] The "Hymne de l'Hyver" here should be mentioned. Although it received its initial impetus from Folengo, Ronsard reproduced in it the Greek outlook on life in some of its most telling aspects.

the onlooker up and down — as it were — a cosmos of indefinite size. Similar in its proportions although different in mould and tenor is the "Hymne des daimons" [168] that arises in the main from a Byzanto-Christian exegesis. Eminently intellectual in its approach, the original offers only flashes of imagery. With the help of Neoplatonic theories Ronsard built from this material an integrated universe that fascinates the eye by its subtle and mysterious materiality. The "Hymne des estoilles" and the "Hymne des astres" associate with astrology and remind of the solemn poeto-scientific character of celestioal charts found in fifteenth and sixteenth century cosmographies. They offer a universe of tremendous size that involves the spheres and implies the body of the earth although the latter appears shrouded in darkness. It is inspired by Marullo [169] and perhaps Manilius [170] whose pictorial force is rare among Roman authors. Unique in this group is the "Hymne du ciel," [171] a poetic image of great serenity that depicts in the main the Ptolemaic universe seen as a sublime mechanism within empty space.

Variety here materializes most distinctly by human and anthropomorphic figures, and its relation to space here too is characteristic of the artistic principle of each opus. Sometimes the individuals depicted are separated from essential spatial matter yet help to define it by the variety of their motions. Sometimes the figures are inextricably bound to the body of the universe. In exceptional cases humanlike figures are altogether absent and diversity then materializes through natural phenomena.

For an example of these vistas the "Ode à Michel de l'Hospital" will here be discussed in detail. It is marked by great pictorial clarity, a fact that strikes the eye if we compare it to its most important source, to Hesiod's *Theogony*, that set Ronsard's mind to motion altogether. [172] In Hesiod gods and nature melt into one. Matter for the Greek poet has metaphysical attributes and fills him with a re-

---

[168] Pierre de Ronsard, *Hymne des daimons,* ed. Albert-Marie Schmidt (Paris, s.d.).

[169] Marullus, *Hymni,* lib. II, "Stellis."

[170] *Astron.,* IV, 122-290.

[171] Henri Franchet, *Le poète et son œuvre d'après Ronsard* (Paris, 1923), p. 199 et seq.

[172] Isidore Silver, *Ronsard and the Greek Epic,* St. Louis, Mo., 1961, pp. 311-318.

ligious shudder. [173] Ronsard, who as a Christian distinguishes between the spiritual and the temporal, cannot comprehend fully the pagan poet. Except for a few images faithfully copied from the Greek original, he neatly separates the material world from the deity. A water-nymph in Ronsard beautifies and enchants its abode, yet remains as a supernatural reality distinct from it, just as in scenes depicting the nativity the figure of the Christ child and the angels give divine brilliance to the earthly image of the stable without sharing with them their identity. As a result Ronsard does not have the elementary force of Hesiod, but he does have, due to the separation of gods and nature, great visual distinctness, well defined outlines and easily discernible detail. He is picturesque.

With regard to its spatial effects the poem contains three large tableaux (vss. 13-126, 183-216, 217-318), [174] all borrowed from the *Theogony*. The first shows the birth of the Muses at the foot of Olympus and their descent to the bottom of the ocean, where they were to meet Jupiter, their father. The second describes the Titans in their underground prison, in Tartarus. The third deals with the war between the gods and the Titans in the heights. The succession of images shows a fine feeling for rhythm and equilibrium. [175] The line of composition moves from heaven downward, stays for a while below, then moves up again towards the sky. The structure not only has shape and continuity, it also has a good distribution of weight. With two light images enclosing a heavy one the object as a whole has balance: it is solid in the middle and it hovers at its two ends.

Studied within its own right as to its spatial effects, the first tableau imparts a feeling of distance through light effects in the sky and through motion in the air and under the sea. In the beginning the author gives a natural background to the figure of Mnemosyne at the time of her pregnancy and the moment when she gave birth to the Muses:

> Memoyre royne d'Eleuthere,
> Par neuf baisers qu'elle receut

---

[173] *Ibid.*, p. 311. Paula Philippson, Genealogie als mythische Form (Oslo, 1936), pp. 6-8.

[174] A number of smaller and less striking images were left out.

[175] Ronsard changed Hesiod's chronological account by placing the punishment of the Titans ahead of their defeat by the gods. He evidently found his own order more poetic.

De Juppiter qui la fist mere,
En neuf soirs neuf filles conceut.
Mais quant la Lune vagabonde
Eut courbé douze fois en rond,
(Pour r'emflammer l'obscur du monde)
La double voulte de son front:
Elle adonc lassement oultrée
Dessoubz Olympe se coucha,
Et criant Lucine, acoucha
De neuf Filles d'une ventrée.

(III, pp. 119-120)

It was Ronsard's idea to evoke here the image of the moon, and he added thereby to the beauty of the Hesiodic text. With its pale and wondrous light the moon serves to create a feeling of remoteness that fits the enigma of the birth of the Muses. Stress on the wanderings of the moon, its nightly appearance and disappearance in the dark sky make the cosmic scene dramatic.

After this introduction, Mnemosyne is seen diving into the ocean with her daughters, an excellent bit of imagery with tremendous spatial repercussions that reach upward to the sky and downward into the depth of the sea. By way of comparison with the plunging figure of Mnemosyne the author throws two images into the air:

Disant ainsi d'un plein saut
Toute dans les eaux s'allonge,
Comme un Cygne qui se plonge
Quand il voit l'aigle d'en-haut,
Ou ainsi que l'arc des Cieux
Qui d'un grand tour spacieux
Tout d'un coup en la mer glisse,
Quand Junon haste ses pas
Pour aller porter là-bas
Un message à sa nourrice. [176]

Mnemosyne's diving evokes the picture of a swan disappearing in the waves at the sight of an eagle; superimposed is the cosmic curve of the second comparison that shows Iris the rainbow, a messanger of Juno, hurrying accross the horizon and sliding into the sea. [177]

---

[176] Ronsard, *Œuvres complètes* (Paris, 1950), I, 388-389; *v.* footnote 162.
[177] Ronsard here uses a Homeric image (*Il.* 24, 77).

To intimate the immenseness of the ocean, the author shows it on the one hand with a magnificent Vergilian hyperbole [178] rising to the sky in a state of turmoil; on the other he hints at its depth, an abyss that swallows a body immersed in it:

> L'eau qui jallit jusques aux cieulx...
> ... ... les avala
> Dedans le gouffre de sa gorge
>
> (III, pp. 124-125)

Just as flight permits one to perceive of height, the sinking of an object to the bottom of the ocean evokes depth. The behavior of the element thereby plays an important part: it opposes the invading body, yet receives it, an almost absurd mixture of materiality and void, an abyss with strong elements of resistance. Mnemosyne is seen advancing in the water with armstrokes; she fathoms, says Ronsard "Le creux du plus humide espace" "Qu'à coups de braz elle fendoit" (III, p. 124). The contrast here is between the substantive "creux" and the verb "fendre." The goddess splits a hollow, the tremendous cavity of the sea that devours her. Slightly different, but altogether similar in its effect is the descent of the Muses into the sea:

> En cent façons, de mains ouvertes,
> Et de piedz voultez en deux pars,
> Sillonoient les Campagnes vertes
> De leurs braz vaguement epars.
> Comme le plomb, dont la secousse
> Treine le filet jusqu'au fond,
> Le desir qui les pousse & pousse
> Avale contre bas leur front.
>
> (III, p. 125)

The likening of the impact of the figures on the sea to a plowing of fields underlines the denseness of the water, whereas in the verb *avaler* [179] the opposite force, the downward drive into the depth, is once more apparent. The simile that evokes a lead-line sinking to the bottom of the sea gives continuity to motion and thereby a more complete image of the distance to be represented.

---

[178] *Aeneid,* I, 103.

[179] The verb *avaler* here is used in its prevalent sixteenth century sense of *faire descendre.*

For another kind of spatial adventure the second tableau describes
regions underneath the surface of the earth. As a presentation of
depth the passage links up thematically with the previous one, but
the medium, the mood, the conditions of light and the conception
of the volume are new. The outstanding motif here is obscurity, an
immense area of deep and sinister darkness.

Following the Hesiodic text, Ronsard first defines the position of
Tartarus: a brazen anvil thrown from Olympus would take nine days
and nine nights to reach the earth; this is half of the distance from
heaven to the beginning of hell, a gaping gulf and a mystery altogether:

> Là de la terre, et là de l'onde
> Sont les racines jusqu'au fond
> De l'abysme la plus profonde
> De cest Orque le plus profond. [180]

The abyss is covered by a triple layer of darkness, says Ronsard
(III, p. 129) reproducing a tantalizing image found in Hesiod. [181] It
is based on the belief that Tartarus is far below the earth and that
whoever wanted to enter it would have to pass through a $\mu\acute{\epsilon}\gamma\alpha$ $\chi\acute{\alpha}\sigma\mu\alpha$,
a big yawning hollow, filled with impenetrable obscurity stacked up
vertically in three strata, and in which a terrible whirlwind would
hurl about any object within reach. [182] More than elsewhere physics
here mingles with metaphysics. Tartarus whose bottom in Greek ways
of thinking is supposed to be equidistant with the firmament from
the surface of the earth, is immesaurable. [183] Here are the roots of the
earth and the ocean; here Atlas holds the world on his shoulders
(III, p. 129). Here lies the key to the mystery of the change between
day and night: for light and darkness go in Tartarus to rest. They
flow in and out through its gates each on its turn as they disappear
and reappear in the open. [184]

---

[180] Ronsard, *Œuvres complètes* (Paris, 1950), I, 391; *v.* footnote 162.

[181] Ronsard calls it *un triple tour*: Hesiod spoke of a triple row.

[182] Hans Flach, *Das System des Hesiodischen Theogonie* (Leipzig, 1874),
p. 123.

[183] *Ibid.*, p. 119.

[184] This contradicts or bypasses the passage describing the darkness of
Tartarus. Inconsistencies handed down by tradition disturbed neither Hesiod
nor Ronsard.

The third tableau, the war between the gods and Titans, takes us once more into the upper world and is perhaps the largest in scope (III, pp. 131-137). It reaches from the top of mountains that are geographically defined but in the poetic scheme attain mythic proportions, to a point in space where the universe appears as an entity, a structure revealing the essential parts of its framework. The gods fight from Olympus the Titans who are stationed on Mount Othryx. The battle, as it evolves, creates cosmic repercussions: the dust stirred up by the warriors rises to the sky, the mountains resound, the seas tremble, heaven and hell partake in the commotion. Eventually Jupiter's thunderbolt sets the pillars of the world on fire:

> Du feu, les deux pilliers du Monde
> Bruslez jusqu'au fond chanceloyent,
> Le Ciel ardoit, la Terre & l'Onde
> Tous petillantz etinceqoyent.
>
> (III, p. 136)

The fact that Ronsard left this voluminous picture to the end for a greater effect shows the importance of space in his poetic vision.

Variety and profusion, the second point in our analysis, materialize in the prodigious number of mythological, historical and semi-historical figures the author depicts while unfolding his spatial imagery. No less than seventy individuals mentioned by name or forming conventional groups appear on the canvass throughout the whole of the poem, and out of these about fourty belong to the three large sceneries here under discussion.

Their expressions, their motions and their general design harmoniously fit or even enhance the three components of the poem. The axis of the first section, a vertical image as a whole, that goes from Olympus down to the bottom of the sea, is stressed and to some extent created by the downward motion of Mnemosyne and the Muses. The second vista, dealing with Tartarus, has a quality of immobility and materiality expressed with equal force by the earth and the powerful and motionless figures of Atlas, the Titans and their guards. In the last scene nature and the individuals meet in a turmoil.

Multitudinousness and diversity reach their climax in the Titanomachy (III, pp. 131-137). The passage well illustrates the difference between Hesiod and Ronsard. In the former gods and nature form more of a unity and the image conveys a natural catastrophe rather than a carefully observed battle scene. Ronsard describes a veritable campaigne, visualizes a motley crowd of men at arms and examines their fighting in the diversity of its detail. [185] He lines them up, describing with relish their special weapons and armor. Jupiter, his chest covered with a magic goatskin, holds on his arms a thunderbolt red with lightning. Mars has a buckler, Vulcan a jawbone in his hand, Apollo and Diana each a bow. On Bellona's head sits Medusa, who looks gruff, growls and spits fire. Styx, the daughter of Ocean, has her arms, legs and breast covered with a black armor. The Titans have their own peculiar arms. [186] Mimas and Rhoetus break the inside of rocks to be thrown and Typhos uses for a lance a fir-tree he uprooted. Ronsard gets his description of gods and half-gods from most everywhere, from Homer, Horace, Pindar Hesiod and others. A Renaissance man, he thrives on richness, and as the fighting develops, he finds a new source of diversity in the changing fortunes of the battle. This aspect of the description in entirely his own. More than elsewhere the graphic power of Hesiod gives room to the picturesqueness of Ronsard. Hercules menaces Rhoetus, but is forced to retreat when Mimas hurls a rock at him. Neptune attacks Typhos, and Apollo who made Enceladus stuble, loses his bow when struck by a rock thrown by Porphyrio. A mighty gesture of Jupiter puts and end to the shifting fortune of the battle. The author describes him as bending down and throwing his fiery missile with arms atretched high. A forceful image was needed to put an end to so much diversity.

Th "Ode à Michel de l'Hospital" may not be the most beautiful of Ronsard's cosmic poems. The natural scenary of the "Hymne de l'hyver" is more striking. The astronomical images found in the "Hymne du ciel" and the "Hymne des estoilles" are more solemn and moving. The "Hymne des daimons" is more imaginative. But none is as lucidly drawn as the great ode about the Muses.

---

[185] Ronsard has drawn to some extent on the more circumstantial description of the Titanomachy of Horace (*Carm.*, III, iv, 53-65).

[186] There is some confusion in the text between Titans and giants.

CONCLUSION

AN ECLIPSE OF THE EXTERNAL WORLD
GUEZ DE BALZAC

Seventeenth century intellectuality puts an end to the sensualism of the Renaissance. Visual variety becomes offensive because of its stress on the physical aspect of life and because it does not lend itself to the orderly presentation that appeals to analytical minds. It tends to be replaced by duality because duality permits focusing on the meaning of a theme; parallelisms and contrasts have great interpretative force. Thus baroque painters create dramatic contrasts between foreground and background or between light and shadow. The dialogue, another form of duality, also serves to interpret a reality in its relief. The composition of baroque paintings often centers around the social intercourse of two or just a few individuals. In the same way literary imagery is marked by the preference of many authors for duality as a form of expression. Such genres as the epistle, essentially a dialogue, or the drama, based on both dialogue and conflict, become prominent in this period.

Spatial effects too are modified under the influence of intellectuality. The theoretical prevails over the visual approach to a cosmos that has become infinite and therefore no longer attractive to the eye. Pascal's "Disproportion de l'homme" [187] develops a universe based essentially on a system, the principle of growth and decline, the increase of objects towards the infinite and their decrease to nothingness. The interest of the description depends on an idea. Descartes's universe is invisible altogether. [188]

---

[187] *Pensées,* ed. Lafuma (Paris, 1951), XV, 199.
[188] *v.* footnote 19.

Beautiful are natural scenes that express the anti-sensual trend by restraint, the toning down of large spatial effects. The hazy background of certain landscapes of Claude Lorrain and the sparse light sometimes found in Poussin reveal this attitude. In literature it is evident in the poems of Maynard, Racan and Théophile and in the prose descriptions of nature of Guez de Balzac.

Balzac is of exceptional interest. His landscapes are marked by an almost neurotic aversion to bright colors and broad illumination. The perspective is vague and airy, and distances are often avoided by natural barriers which increase the intimacy of the vista. Balzac's air is thin, the beauty of objects depicted depends on their slight corporeality. There is little motion in his sceneries. The tranquility of the outer world fills his soul with serenity and peace. It is nature toned down in all its aspects. Yet the tableau is a full experience. And when surrounded by a paradise of vague and sheltered areas, of self-effacing shapes, and of unobtrusive colors, the author's mind is at rest.

At the beginning of a letter to La Motte Aigron he describes a cloudy day with an overwhelming affection: "Il fit hier un de ces jours sans Soleil, que vous dites qui semblent à ceste belle aveugle, dont Philippe second estoit amoureux. Veritablement, je n'eus jamais tant de plaisir à m'entretenir moy-mesme...; l'ombre que le Ciel faisoit de tous costez, m'empeschoit de desirer celle des grottes et des forests." [189] Such fondness for darkness is probably unique in literature. The author, his emotions aroused, searches for a poetic interpretation of the phenomenon. An exalted feminine figure of times past arises in his mind, a beautiful blind woman, lady-love of the Spanish king Philip I. [190] The image is subtle. As often in the seventeenth century, eyes here are conceived of as a source of light. [191] Balzac

---

[189] *Les premières lettres de Guez de Balzac,* ed. Bibas and Butler (Paris, 1933-34), I, 132.

[190] Balzac refers to the Princess of Eboly, who was actually one-eyed as a result of a childhood accident. Let us observe that she hardly fits the mood of the landscape. Far from being soft, she was self-willed, temperamental, voluptuous and occasionally vulgar. A mistress of Antonio Perez, she, together with her lover, was persecuted by the king, whose affection for her remains, nevertheless, a matter of historical controversy.

[191] "Mais ce que Sapho a de souverainement agréable, c'est qu'elle a les yeux si beaux, si vifs, si amoureux et si pleins d'esprit, qu'on ne peut ni en soutenir l'éclat ni en détacher ses regards. En effet, ils brillent d'un feu si pénétrant..." (Madeleine de Scudéry, *Artamène ou le Grand Cyrus*).

devises the idea of a glowless and very beautiful emanation which spreads from the eyes of a blind woman. It looks down upon the earth and covers it with pale, enchanted rays. Her glance is identified with the woman herself, as if her whole being would materialize in it. The beauty of her visual expression stands for the beauty of the woman as a whole. The author reveals how dark the cloudy day thus described actually is by saying that the shadow cast by the sky stopped him from seeking that of the grottos and forests.

From the description of the scenery at large we are led to a particular spot where the obscurity is even denser:

> Je ne veux pas vous faire le portraict d'une maison, dont l'ouvrage n'est ny si excellent que de Fontainebleau, ny la matiere si precieuse que le marbre & le porphyre; Je vous dirai seulement qu'à la porte il y a un bois, où en plein midy il n'entre de jour que ce qu'il en faut pour n'estre pas nuict, & pour empescher que toutes les couleurs ne soient noires. Tellement que de l'obscurité & de la lumiere il se fait un troisiesme temps, qui peut estre supporté des yeux des malades, & cacher les defauts des femmes qui sont fardées. Les arbres y sont verds jusqu'à la racine, tant de leurs propres feuilles, que de celles du lierre qui les embrasse... [192]

Balzac's country-house and the adjacent forest appeared at first to the reader as part of a larger scene. The author now shows the forest from within. He is evidently delighted at having woods in front of his home. When he leaves his dwelling his first contact with nature is in semi-darkness. The place is obscure. The sun's rays, sifted and attenuated by the foliage, hardly permit us to discern colors. The only color the author shows us is the green of the leaves and of the ivy which covers the trees and roots. It is undoubtedly a deep green which, far from enlivening the scene, merely adds variety to the darkness and increases its magic. The duskiness reigning in the forest is even and consistent, an optical condition of a special sort that can be called neither light nor darkness. Its softness pleases and flatters the senses. It soothes the eyes of the sick and hides the shortcomings of feminine cosmetics. It is a source of physical well-being and of beauty.

---

[192] *Op. cit.*, pp. 133-34.

At this point the picture brightens. The author had walked out of the forest, and flowers and sunshine emerge on the canvas. What actually happens is that Balzac proceeds to the description of another day, or rather, from a particular day he recalled, to any day at all. Of course, the literary landscapist has the privilege of wandering in space and time, presenting within the same composition vistas observed from different spots on different days. Yet there is harmony between such heterogeneous parts of Balzac's tableau. Since sunny passages contain restrained light, they enliven the dark ones without disrupting the artistic equilibrium as a whole. The dimly lit and obscure surfaces illustrate the same principle; they are two different tones of the same scale. And, characteristically, where the sensuous experience increases, the author becomes more fearful of excesses. His struggle against them becomes more emphatic. Illumination must be as soothing to his eyes as darkness. A field of flowers, mostly anemones and tulips, has emerged next to the forest: "De là j'entre en una prairie, où je marche sur les tulipes & les anemones, que j'ay fait mesler avec les autres fleurs..." [193] No colors are mentioned; the scene, although rather animated, lacks visual intensity. Thence the author descends into a valley, a place so hidden that nobody else knows of it. It is the most secret part of his desert. In this secluded spot he spends his happiest hours. Its colors are fresh and green. It is crossed by the Charente, which is bordered by trees, and in the waters of which swans are swimming. Very interesting is the description of the sun: "Le Soleil envoye bien de la clarté jesques-là, mais il n'y fait jamais aller de chaleur; le lieu est si bas qu'il ne sçoroit recevoir que les dernieres pointes de ses rayons, qui sont d'autant plus beaux qu'ils ont moins de force, et que leur lumiere est toute pure." [194] For Balzac the sunshine must be lacking "force" in order to reach the climax of its beauty. A tactile experience mingles here with a visual one, and both are based on the same general principle. The cool light, with its lesser glow, soothes the eye, and simultaneously its tepid touch comforts the rest of the body. At this point Balzac enjoys the dimness of the outer world with all his senses.

Let us now review the entire tableau merely from the point of view of its spatial effects. To a certain extent they go hand in hand

---

[193] *Ibid.*, p. 134.
[194] *Ibid.*

with the quality of light. Spatial phenomena turn vague in dim illumination. Yet Balzac finds other means that also lead up to the same goal.

Thus the soft and subdued materiality of the landscape, due in a certain measure to obscurity or restrained light, is enhanced by vague indications of motion, and occasionally by a stress on complete immobility. We have found excellent examples in Lemaire de Belges's or Ronsard's descriptions of how movement can increase the bodily character of objects.[195] Balzac places emphasis on the absence of wind that leaves unruffled the surface of the river. His air is thin, the water does not display its physical potentialities: "Leau de la riviere paroissoit aussi plate que celle d'un lac; & si en pleine mer un tel calme surprenoit pour tousjours les vaisseaux, ils ne pourroient jamais ny se sauver, ny se perdre."[196] This image of ships at sea that does not belong to the main vista but appears by way of interpretation, as it were, on its margin, is very illustrative of Balzac's intentions. The boats can move neither horizontally nor vertically down the sea; the sea is motionless, does not reveal its depth; there is no friction between matter and matter. The complete absence of motion associates with timelessness in the author's mind. He has effaced the sensory characteristics of his objects to a point where they seem to shed their earthly aspect and point towards eternity.

Strong spatial impressions are further avoided by vague indications of distance and sometimes by natural barriers such as mountains. Here again conditions of light play an important part. Under the heavily clouded sky that covers the first part of the scene, remote objects are necessarily dim or altogether invisible. We have mentioned that semi-obscurity makes the author feel as if he were in a "grotto." Dimmer light reduces the area and gives the author a happy feeling of protection. But his scenery has actual boundaries, too. As a whole it is limited by mountains: "Nous sommes icy en un petit rond, tout couronné de montagnes."[197] Particular spots described often are very cozy. In the forest that is in front of Balzac's house and that is seen

---

[195] Jean Lemaire de Belges, *Illustrations de Gaule et Singularitez de Troie*, I, Chap. 28. Ronsard, "Ode à Michel de l'Hospital," *Œuvres complètes* (Paris, 1914-67), III, 118-163.

[196] *Op. cit.*, p. 132.

[197] *Ibid.*, p. 133.

most of the time from within, visual limitation reaches its climax. When leaving the woods and entering the flowery meadow referred to, we seem to be for a short while in the open. Then the author takes us down to his valley: "Je descens aussi quelquefois dans ceste valée, qui est la plus secrete partie de mon desert, & qui jusques icy n'avoit esté connuë de personne. C'est un païs à souhaiter & à peindre, que j'ay choisi pour vacquer à mes plus cheres occupations, & passer les plus douces heures de ma vie ... Les cygnes qui couvroient autrefois toute la riviere se sont retirez en ce lieu de seureté." [198] The place is not only enclosed but practically hidden from the outer world; hence it is a supreme source of happiness for Balzac. To impress upon us the charm and allurement found in such seclusion, he tells us a story of swans who used to spread all along the river, and, in search of shelter, eventually withdrew into his enchanted valley.

It is noteworthy that at a certain point of his description Balzac's thoughts turn from outer life to his inner world. He observes the effect of the countryside on his state of mind. The study of the relationship between nature and ego is often found in literary landscapes, each time of course, with an intimate significance of its own. Very characteristically, it serves here to intellectualize the imagery, to reduce further its sensuous aspects, thereby deepening and ennobling it. As in other 17th century writings, the soul pervades physical realities, to sublimate and to dim them. At a certain moment the whole landscape turns into pure thought and seems to illustrate a mental reality.

A moral principle has evolved from the description of nature. When approaching the river and the valley so described, the most talkative people become silent and turn into dreamers. Balzac himself is always happy there: "Pour peu que je m'y arreste, il me semble que je retourne en ma premiere innocence. Mes desirs, mes craintes, & mes esperances cessent tout d'un coup; Tous les mouvemens de mon ame se relaschent, & je n'ay point de passions, ou si j'en ay, je les gouverne comme des bestes apprivoisées." [199] The passage contains a somewhat complex notion of happiness. The idea of bliss found in the absence of strong emotions reminds of an aspect of Epicurean

---

[198] *Ibid.,* p. 134.
[199] *Ibid.*

ethics,[200] whereas the search for happiness through the control of passions suggests Descartes's *Traité des passions*. This latter concept is a key to the relationship between thought and landscape. Passions arise from the senses and must be restrained by the soul, according to Descartes. The absense of strong sensuous perceptions leads Balzac to his artistic beauty and inner equilibrium.

There is a description of nature contained in the introduction to Balzac's *Le Prince* that derives from a similar artistic concept. Somewhat brighter and more fluid as a whole, its particular charm consists in gentle contrasts between slight opacity and soft illumination, and the imaginative presentation of spatial restraint.

The moral idea, similar to the one discussed above, is present at the beginning. The author's natural surroundings fill his soul with serenity and a mild sort of happiness. He is gay without being excited. Free from agitation, a state comparable to pain, he has all the pleasures joy may impart. He knows neither fear nor hope; all his passions are at rest. More emphatically than in the letter to De La Motte, the concept of happiness is here mingled with that of virtue. Under such circumstances, suspicion, envy, and hatred are absent from man's soul.[201]

Instead of a foggy day, the author here presents a clear autumn day. His genuine fondness for nature in a state of decline is almost startling: "I'ay esté assez long-temps dans le monde, mais je n'ay vescu qu'autant que dura l'Automne passé: El pource qu'il n'est pas possible de faire revenir ces jours bien-heureux, et qui me furent si chers, je tasche le plus que je puis de les regouster par le souvenir, et par le discours... La pureté de l'air, que je commençois à respirer, et que je recevois avidement, comme une nourriture, qui m'estoit nouvelle; et la face riante de la campagne, qui monstroit encore sur soy une partie de ses biens, et se paroit de derniers presens qu'elle

---

[200] Cf. for a similar reaction to Epicurism Pierre de Charron, *De la sagesse livres trois* (Bordeaux, 1601, II, Chap. 38: Selon eux [les Epicuriens] le n'avoir poinct de mal est le plus heureux bien estre que l'homme puisse esperer icy. *Nimium boni est cui nihil est mali.* Cecy est comme un milieu ou neutralité entre la volupté prise au sens premier & commun; & la douleur, c'est comme jadis le sein d'Abraham entre le paradis & lefer des damnez. C'est un estat & une assiette douce & paisible, une aequable constante & arreté volupté, qui ressemble aucunement l'euthimie & tranquilité d'esprit, estimée le souverain bien par les Philosophes..."

[201] Guez de Balzac, *Œuvres*, ed. Moreau, I, 7-8.

devoit faire aux hommes, me donnoient des pensées si douces et si
tranquilles ..." [202] Balzac simply extolls scarcity. What he loves in the
countryside is that it shows only "part of its wealth" that is adorned
with the "last presents" it has to offer.

Even in describing the fall, Balzac chooses those parts of the day
in which the sunlight is mildest. He depicts the morning and the
evening. The morning scene offers delicate contrasts between light and
shadow mixed with faint indications of corporeality and motion:

> Et à la verité quand nous eussions eu durant cette saison la
> direction du monde, et que nous eussions fait nous-mesmes
> les jours, nous n'en pouvions pas avoir de plus beaux, ny
> dispenser l'ombre et la lumiere, le froid et le chaud avec
> une plus égale mesure. Il s'eslevoit bien quelquefois une pe-
> tite vapeur de la riviere voisine, qui l'envelopoit comme dans
> un ré, et s'espandoit sur la superficie de la Terre: Mais outre
> qu'elle n'attendoit pas tousjours le Soleil pour se défaire,
> et qu'elle n'en pouvoit soustenir les premiers rayons, elle
> n'avoit jamais tant de force qu'elle montast à la hauteur de
> nos plus basses fenestres, et nous jouïssions d'un calme tres-
> net, et d'une clarté extremement vive pendant qu'il y avoit
> un peu de trouble et de fumée au dessous de nous. [203]

There is some contrast between the tender sunbeams that descend
from the sky and the mist that has arisen at dawn from the river.
This conflict is kept down to a minimum. The sun has no force; the
fog lacks density, its obscurity is unobstrusive. It has a vague bodily
character which attracts Balzac's eye. It envelops the river "like a
net," he says, and then spreads on the surface of the earth. A hazy
sort of motion arises thereby on the landscape. It is hardly discernible, then stops altogether. The fog does not have the strength to
rise to the lowest windows of Balzac's home; as the morning pro-
gresses, it tends to disappear.

The day at its height does not attract the author. He spends the
noon hours and the afternoon in his home talking to friends or
reading. Twilight lures him out of his house again: "Mais le declin
du jour s'approchant, et ce qui restoit de sa chaleur n'estant pas plus
difficile à supporter que la vapeur d'un bain tiede, je montois ordi-

---

[202] *Ibid.*
[203] *Ibid.,* pp. 8-9.

nairement à cheval, et sortois du logis." [204] Through a corridor of mulberry trees he reaches the Charente, possibly the same region he had described in his letter to De La Motte Aigron, although this time it presents somewhat different aspects. Here Balzac sits and waits for the sunset, a spectacle he never misses.

With regard to coloring and light, the following passage is a curious mixture of vividness and restraint. In one way it is the liveliest image we have in Balzac, yet the author's predilection for restraint here is more apparent than elsewhere. He admires the sunset because of "cette riche effusion de couleurs qu'il verse en se retirant, et dans laquelle il semble qu'il tempere ses rayons pour les rendre supportables et qu'il adoucit sa lumiere pour espargner nostre veuë." [205] Balzac sees and here enjoys an abundance of colors. He does not specify them, to be sure, as would Ronsard or Belleau, yet he succeeds in evoking the phenomenon before our eyes. But immediately he sets about to efface its sensuous impact. The beauty of the colors depends on their lack of luminosity. They have arisen from an effort of the sun, so to speak, to temper its glow and soothe our eyes. With all their variety they are by their very essence an expression of restraint. They are a manifestation of nature at its decline — the last present of a dying day in a dying season.

The spatial effects of the evening scene are marked by the familiar and here particularly fascinating struggle against substance and distance. The Charente is surrounded by hills so steep that the trees do not seem to have any hold on them. They give the impression of being attached to or even of climbing on the slopes: "Et la pente en estant fort droite, vous diriez que les arbres n'y sont pas plantez, mais qu'on les y a attachez, ou qu'ils y grimpent, tant ils y ont peu de prise. [206] A remarkable observation. The author's eyes are highly sensitive to any detail that serves to reduce the materiality of objects. Firmly rooted trees suggest sturdiness; their tenuous contact with the ground makes them les substantial. From another point of view, the hills here described which enclose the scene increase its intimacy. At one point this coziness reaches a sort of climax. The river narrows down to such an extent that the mulberry trees surrounding it join

---

[204] *Ibid.*, p. 9.
[205] *Ibid.*, p. 10.
[206] *Ibid.*

their branches, forming a bower so perfect that it seems to be formed on purpose. [207]

And then comes what this critic considers the outstanding sentence in the text. While Balzac waits for the sunset, his eyes rest on the surface of the water: "La ... i'avois le plaisir de regarder au fonds de l'eau les choses qui se passoient dedans l'air, et de voir nager tout ce qui voloit." [208] The author reaches here the height of self-expression. Carried away by enthusiasm, he creates a mirage which in its artistic emotionalism equals the opposite ideal of the Renaissance. We have seen that the 16th century passionately observed the sky. It searched for depth, distance, and body and tried to retain all that moved and stirred in the open spaces. Since then the physical universe has lost its charm. Seemingly an infinite monster, it led Pascal, who looked at it squarely, to despair. Balzac the artist turns his back on it and reproduces it in an enchanted mirror, where, devoid of its awesome vastness, it is again agreeable to look at. With a single ingenious and fanciful device, he reduces volume, plasticity and motion: he looks at the world in its reflection on the calm flat surface of the water. With the transformation of three-dimensional flight to a two-dimensional plane, the concept of restraint turns, by means of an optical illusion, into magic. It is the *fata morgana* of the seventeenth century.

---

[207] *Ibid.*
[208] *Ibid.*

NORTH CAROLINA STUDIES IN THE
ROMANCE LANGUAGES AND LITERATURES

I.S.B.N. Prefix 0-88438

Recent Titles

Recent Titles

THE TEACHINGS OF SAINT LOUIS. A CRITICAL TEXT, by David O'Connell. 1972. (No. 116). *-916-2.*

HIGHER, HIDDEN ORDER: DESIGN AND MEANING IN THE ODES OF MALHERBE, by David Lee Rubin. 1972. (No. 117). *-917-0.*

JEAN DE LE MOTE "LE PARFAIT DU PAON," édition critique par Richard J. Carey. 1972. (No. 118). *-918-9.*

CAMUS' HELLENIC SOURCES, by Paul Archambault. 1972. (No. 119). *-919-7.*

FROM VULGAR LATIN TO OLD PROVENÇAL, by Frede Jensen. 1972. (No. 120). *-920-0.*

GOLDEN AGE DRAMA IN SPAIN: GENERAL CONSIDERATION AND UNUSUAL FEATURES, by Sturgis E. Leavitt. 1972. (No. 121). *-921-9.*

THE LEGEND OF THE "SIETE INFANTES DE LARA" (*Refundición toledana de la crónica de 1344* versión), study and edition by Thomas A. Lathrop. 1972. (No. 122). *-922-7.*

STRUCTURE AND IDEOLOGY IN BOIARDO'S "ORLANDO INNAMORATO," by Andrea di Tommaso. 1972. (No. 123). *-923-5.*

STUDIES IN HONOR OF ALFRED G. ENGSTROM, edited by Robert T. Cargo and Emmanuel J. Mickel, Jr. 1972. (No. 124). *-924-3.*

A CRITICAL EDITION WITH INTRODUCTION AND NOTES OF GIL VICENTE'S "FLORESTA DE ENGANOS," by Constantine Christopher Stathatos. 1972. (No. 125). *-925-1.*

LI ROMANS DE WITASSE LE MOINE. *Roman du treizième siècle.* Édité d'après le manuscrit, fonds français 1553, de la Bibliothèque Nationale, Paris, par Denis Joseph Conlon. 1972. (No. 126). *-926-X.*

EL CRONISTA PEDRO DE ESCAVIAS. *Una vida del Siglo XV,* por Juan Bautista Avalle-Arce. 1972. (No. 127). *-927-8.*

AN EDITION OF THE FIRST ITALIAN TRANSLATION OF THE "CELESTINA," by Kathleen V. Kish. 1973. (No. 128). *-928-6.*

MOLIÈRE MOCKED. THREE CONTEMPORARY HOSTILE COMEDIES: *Zélinde, Le portrait du peintre, Élomire Hypocondre,* by Frederick Wright Vogler. 1973. (No. 129). *-929-4.*

C.-A. SAINTE-BEUVE. *Chateaubriand et son groupe littéraire sous l'empire.* Index alphabétique et analytique établi par Lorin A. Uffenbeck. 1973. (No. 130). *-930-8.*

THE ORIGINS OF THE BAROQUE CONCEPT OF "PEREGRINATIO," by Juergen Hahn. 1973. (No. 131). *-931-6.*

THE "AUTO SACRAMENTAL" AND THE PARABLE IN SPANISH GOLDEN AGE LITERATURE, by Donald Thaddeus Dietz. 1973. (No. 132). *-932-4.*

FRANCISCO DE OSUNA AND THE SPIRIT OF THE LETTER, by Laura Calvert. 1973. (No. 133). *-933-2.*

ITINERARIO DI AMORE: DIALETTICA DI AMORE E MORTE NELLA Vita Nuova, by Margherita De Bonfils Templer. 1973. (No. 134). *-934-0.*

Symposia

LOS NARRADORES HISPANOAMERICANOS DE HOY, edited by Juan Bautista Avalle-Arce. 1973. (No. 1). *-951-0.*

When ordering please cite the *ISBN Prefix* plus the last four digits for each title.

Send orders to:

International Scholarly Book Service, Inc.
P.O. Box 4347
Portland, Oregon 97208
U.S.A.

www.ingramcontent.com/pod-product-compliance
Lightning Source LLC
Chambersburg PA
CBHW020918180526
45163CB00007B/2783